The Sadness of Christ

And Final Prayers and Instructions

by

Saint Thomas More

Edited with an Introduction
by Gerard Wegemer

*English Translation
by Clarence Miller*

Scepter Publishers
Princeton, NJ

The translation of *The Sadness of Christ* is taken with permission from *Complete Works of St. Thomas More*, Volume 14, *De Tristitia Christi*, Library of Congress No. 63-7949. © 1976, Yale University Press.

ISBN No. 0-933932-66-9

First Printing, 1993
Second Printing, August 1994
Third Printing, July 1995

© 1993 Scepter Publishers, Inc.
Printed in the United States of America

CONTENTS

INTRODUCTION

T HE FULL TITLE of this book—*The Sadness, the Weariness, the Fear, and the Prayer of Christ Before He Was Taken Prisoner*—focuses sharply on Christ's human reaction to His approaching death. By doing so, this title suggests an apparent paradox in Christ's life. As More points out, Christ "taught His disciples not to be afraid of those who kill the body only"; so "how can it be fitting that He Himself should . . . be very much afraid of those same persons. . . ?" (8). More draws out the difficulties even further by recalling those martyrs who "rushed to their deaths eagerly and joyfully." How is it appropriate, he asks, "that Christ Himself, the very prototype and leader of martyrs, the standard bearer of them all, should be so terrified at the approach of pain, so shaken, so utterly downcast?" (8) — so sad?

Since *The Sadness of Christ* is More's last work and one that he heavily revised, we may well find ourselves wondering why he chose the unusual focus and form of this book. At first glance, *The Sadness* may appear to be a rather ordinary and somewhat matter-of-fact Gospel commentary. Yet a good Gospel commentary is not something ordinary, and the matter-of-fact facade is an important part of More's design. After all, what he writes applies pointedly to individuals of his own age who were responsible for the virtual destruction of the Church in England. He writes of the apostles' falling asleep and of Judas' betrayal of Christ as "a mirror image . . . of what has happened through the ages" (46). Peter, James, and John represent Church leaders who fall asleep at their post, while the Jewish leaders who commissioned Judas represent "other governors and other caesars" who rise against Christ's followers — governors and caesars such as Thomas Cromwell and Henry VIII. Hence one can appreciate the prudent indirection that characterizes this book. But More's message is not limited to the issues of his own time. Intentionally universal, it is applicable to every age and to every individual.

More gives his own summary of the chief subject matter of this book as "the story of that time when the apostles were sleeping as the Son of Man was being betrayed." Here he sees "a mysterious image of future times" (61). In this brief garden scene that takes place after the Last Supper, More finds a lesson for all time — a lesson so important that Christ decided to reveal it in detail after the Resurrection (31-32).

If we the readers are to discover and profit from this lesson, More requires that we strive to exercise just those qualities that emerge as the book's principal themes: alertness and patience. To use the refrain of the book: we must be patient enough to "get up, stay awake, and not fall asleep."

The Sadness of Christ begins with a paragraph that immediately introduces More's purpose: to contrast Christ's way of acting with our own. For example, Christ's tabletalk is edifying, whereas ours is "not only meaningless and inconsequential" but even vicious; and while Christ sings a hymn of thanksgiving, "we leave the table without giving thanks to God for the banquets He has bestowed upon us, with never a thought for the gratitude we owe Him" (1).

More then gives a brief explanation of his own principles for interpreting the Bible. Every word is inspired and carries multiple levels of meaning. Even the names of the stream Christ crosses (Cedron, "sadness") and the garden he enters (Gethsemane, "most fertile valley") carry veiled and mysterious meanings "which attentive men, with the help of the Holy Spirit, would try to uncover" (3). Here lies the importance of this short commentary: it shows how More the saintly lawyer read Scripture, giving clear evidence of a lifetime's reflection.

In what is often an extraordinarily hard-hitting commentary, More gives his final warning and instruction, which might be summed up in the dominant metaphor and message of the book: Don't fall asleep in times of temptation. Sadness, weariness, and fear are presented as strong temptations faced by good-willed people in their struggle to do good; these temptations are experienced by everyone as part of the human condition, including Christ Himself. More's prescription for such temptations is simple; it is the one repeatedly given by Christ each time He returns to ask His closest apostles to watch with Him: Stay awake by praying. One might well object that it is natural to fall asleep when we are tired or discouraged. Yes, admits More, it may be natural, but often it is also sinful — so sinful that one can end up in hell.

Patience could well be seen as the ultimate lesson of this commentary on Christ's agony and capture. "Patience," of course, comes from the same root as "passion," both meaning "to suffer"; and More recognized that the greatest sources of suffering are the people closest to us. The book ends with a reminder and a warning: a reminder that each soul is won by patience (101); a warning that patience is so "difficult and arduous a virtue" and requires "such a lofty peak of heroic virtue" that even Christ's hand-picked apostles fell short (104).

To help us understand the difficulties of patience, More uses a common metaphor that gradually acquires the most powerful of meanings: our tendency to fall asleep when we should not. One of the most moving portions of this book is Christ's encounter with His closest disciples after they ignore His plea to keep Him company during His hour of greatest suffering. Three times He returns to ask for their vigilance, and all three times they fall asleep. When Christ repeatedly asks, "Why did you fall asleep?" attentive readers know that the question is directed to them as well.

When Christ finds His apostles asleep for the third time, More marvels that "Judas the traitor at the same time was so wide awake and intent on betraying the Lord that the very idea of sleep never entered his head" (46). He then goes on to make some of the most pointed comments of the whole book. He asks:

> Does not this contrast between the traitor and the apostles present to us a clear and sharp mirror image (as it were), a sad and terrible view of what has happened through the ages from those times even to our own? Why do not bishops contemplate in this scene their own somnolence? Since they have succeeded in the place of the apostles, would that they would reproduce their virtues just as eagerly as they embrace their authority and as faithfully as they display their sloth and sleepiness! For very many are sleepy and apathetic in sowing virtues among the people and maintaining the truth, while the enemies of Christ, in order to sow vices and uproot the faith . . . , are wide awake . . . .(46).

Noting that this apparently innocent act of falling asleep is actually a "mirror image" of what happens in every age, More proceeds to give a rare and extraordinarily strong correction to the apostles' successors.

More is rebuking not just the bishops, however, but all those in positions of leadership. Having been in such positions himself, he is well aware that the weight and sorrow of office can "so grip the mind that its strength is sapped and reason gives up the reins." Such "heavy-hearted sleep" can, indeed, lead one to "neglect to do what the duty of his office requires . . . , like a cowardly ship's captain who is so disheartened by the furious din of a storm that he deserts the helm, hides away cowering in some cranny, and abandons the ship to the waves." As strong as this rebuke is up to now, it becomes still stronger, reaching its climax with all the rhetorical force of which a man of More's literary genius is capable: "If a bishop does this, I would certainly not hesitate to juxtapose and compare his sadness with the sadness that leads, as [Paul] says, to hell; indeed, I would consider it far worse, since such sadness in religious matters seems to spring from a mind which despairs of God's help" (47).

Yet how can one keep from falling asleep when burdened by sadness, weariness, and fear? In grappling with this all-important question, one can understand More's careful choice in selecting the topic of his last and, in an essential way, most revealing of all his works. The answer is confident and obedient prayer, as taught by Christ in this particular scene of the Gospel.

In the section on prayer (which begins on p. 17), More shows Christ "face down on the earth," praying that this cup might pass. Calling attention to how "Christ the commander teaches by His own example," More then addresses the reader directly: "Reader, let us pause for a little at this point and contemplate with a devout mind our commander lying on the ground in humble supplication." After this personal appeal for attention, More shows in one of his artistically crafted sentences how the attentive reader will profit from a prayerful meditation on this scriptural passage:

> For if we do this carefully [contemplate Christ prostrate in prayer], a ray of that light which enlightens every man who comes into the world will illuminate our minds so that we will see, recognize, deplore, and at long last correct, I will not say the negligence, sloth, or apathy, but rather the feeblemindedness, the insanity, the downright blockheaded stupidity with which most of us approach the all-powerful God and instead of praying reverently, address Him in a lazy and sleepy sort of way; and by the same token I am very much afraid that instead of placating Him and gaining His favor we exasperate Him and sharply provoke His wrath. (18-19)

What More does in this one sentence is an example of what he does in the book as a whole. He tries to get his reader to see the real meaning of Christ's "ordinary" human actions. If we truly see, we will not be negligent, slothful or apathetic; we will not act downright stupidly; we will not go through life in a lazy and sleepy sort of way.

The whole problem is lack of attention. We let our "thoughts wander wildly during prayers, frantically flitting about in a throng of absurd fantasies" (19). Unlike Christ, who is prostrate before God and wholly absorbed in His prayer, we let "our actions . . . betray that our minds are wandering miles away . . . " (20). With his earthy and humorous irony, More tries to make us see the absurdity of the way we pray. In embarrassing contrast to the way Christ prays, "we scratch our heads, clean our fingernails with a pocketknife, pick our noses with our fingers, meanwhile making the wrong responses." How can we not be "ashamed to pray in such a deranged state of mind and body—to beseech God's favor in a matter so crucial for us . . . ? (20).

What follows is another brilliant image to help us real-

ize the nature of prayer. More suggests that we imagine
we have "committed a crime of high treason" against a
prince who is willing to commute or even suspend the
death penalty if we show ourselves sorry. His irony then
brings into high relief the absurdity of slothful prayer:

> Now when you have been brought into the presence of
> the prince, go ahead and speak to him carelessly, casually,
> without the least concern. . . . Then yawn, stretch, sneeze,
> spit without giving it a thought, and belch up the fumes
> of your gluttony. In short, conduct yourself in such a way
> that he can clearly see from your face, your voice, your
> gestures, and your whole bodily deportment that while
> you are addressing him you are thinking about something
> else. Tell me now, what success could you hope for from
> such a plea as this? (20-21)

More wants us to realize that we would not fall asleep
or be slovenly in our prayer if we actually remembered
what prayer is and to Whom we are speaking in our
prayer.

Peter, James, and John fell asleep "even at the very
time when such an enormous danger was threatening
their loving master," because they had not acquired the
habit of prayer. Unless we are constant in prayer, "our
minds, no matter how willing to do good, are swept back
into the evils of temptation" (27). Christ tells us to pray
because this is absolutely necessary if we are not to give in
to temptation (28).

After revealing the nature of Christ's prayer, More
then focuses upon the extent of Christ's agony: a sadness,
a weariness, a fear so great that it led to the "unprecedented phenomenon" of His sweating blood (32). After
reviewing various reasons for this agony, More observes
that "the very purpose" of this event was to teach "those
whose hearts are troubled" how to bear adversity. The

example of adversity More uses is again the burden of public office, which usually takes the form of sadness, fear, or weariness (33, 47). More seems to present this burden as one of the most dangerous temptations that can face a good person. Experiencing these temptations is not a sin; even Christ in His humanity felt their full weight. Yet one must never stop struggling against them (37, 47, 54-55). "Everyone has sufficient grounds to be afraid that he may grow weary under his burden and give in" (37). But this very tendency should actually cause us "to rouse ourselves and wake up to virtuous living" (36); it should make us more and more convinced of our absolute need for the habit of prayer.

What each of us can do is to avoid the "drowsy position of sitting [that] lets sleep gradually slip up" on us (54). This, however, requires "fighting against sleep. . . . Then once we have cast off idle sleep . . . , life with its eagerness will resume its sway" (54). But what if we do not feel such eagerness in the face of great danger? Here More introduces his reflection on the two types of martyrs: the ones who boldly and joyfully rush to their deaths and the ones who "face death with fear and trembling" (43). He subtly observes that the first kind either has received a special gift of God or else is proud and therefore no martyr at all. Hence, even people of this fearless type should be fearful — of their motives; they should be aware of their own weakness and the power of pride. Hence, "the person who is conscious of his own eagerness needs not so much encouragement to be daring as perhaps a reminder to be afraid lest his presumption, like Peter's, lead to sudden relapse and fall." Faced with persecution and death, most people will "feel anxious, heavy-hearted, fearful." However, "for both sorts of martyrs this anguish of Christ is most salutary: it keeps the one from being over-exultant, and it makes the other be of good hope when his spirit is crestfallen and downcast" (44).

In either case, if one is not to be negligent, if one is not to fall asleep, one must pray. "Again and again He drove home this point to them, that prayer is the only safeguard against temptation and that if someone refuses it entrance into the castle of his soul and shuts it out by yielding to sleep, through such negligence he permits the besieging troops of the devil (that is, temptations to evil) to break in" (55). Christ reminds His apostles repeatedly to get up and pray, immediately warning them "how great the impending danger [is], in order to show that no drowsy or lukewarm prayer [will] suffice. . ." (59).

After this rousing call to vigilance and prayer, Judas comes. In the previous section, Christ showed how to work patiently with the weak but good-willed. By returning three times to ask their help, Christ was appealing to the personal freedom and responsibility of His disciples; eventually, this example of loving friendship would lead each of the eleven remaining apostles to die rather than ever abandon Christ again.

In dealing with Peter, Christ used mild words, but they had a point that was "sharp and piercing" (26). With Judas, He uses a strategy that is in some ways similar but in other ways quite different. Throughout, however, Christ teaches us

to bear patiently and gently all injuries and snares treacherously set for us; not to smolder with anger, not to seek revenge, not to give vent to our feelings by hurling back insults, not to find any empty pleasure in tripping up an enemy through some clever trick, but rather to set ourselves against deceitful injury with genuine courage, to conquer evil with good — in fine, to make every effort by words both gentle and harsh, to insist both in season and out of season, that the wicked may change their ways to

good, so that if anyone should be suffering from a disease
that does not respond to treatment, he may not blame the
failure on our negligence but rather attribute it to the virulence of his own disease. (72-73)

In the case of Judas, More points out how "Christ as a
most conscientious physician tries both ways of effecting a
cure." First He uses gentle words, asking, "Friend, why
have you come?" But when Judas shows no sign of
responding, Christ "immediately adds in a grave tone,
'Judas, do you betray the Son of Man with a kiss?'" (73).
Christ then turns to the crowd and gives a glimpse of His
power by making them all draw back and fall to the
ground.

At this point, More marvels at the change that has
come over Jesus: from one so fearful and sad that He sweat
blood, He has become someone absolutely astonishing for
the "manly courage with which He fearlessly approaches
that whole mass of armed men . . . " (76). These armed
men, along with the leaders who sent them, represent the
brief power of darkness that "'will also be given to other
governors and other caesars against other disciples of
mine'" (100). More sees in this event something perennial
in the struggle for virtue. Christ's disciples will always
meet opposition; however, "'whatever my disciples endure
and whatever they say, they will not endure by their own
strength or say of themselves, but conquering through my
strength they will win their souls by their patience, and it
is my Father's spirit that will speak in them'" (100).

More sees in Christ's agony the most important lesson
that each Christian must come to learn. He has this advice
for those who suffer:

Whoever is utterly crushed by feelings of anxiety and fear
and is tortured by the fear that he may yield to despair, let
him consider this agony of Christ, let him meditate on it

constantly and turn it over in his mind, let him drink deep
and health-giving draughts of consolation from this
spring. (44)

One especially important lesson to learn from this
scene is that prayer works. An angel from heaven comes
to comfort Christ, and He can display "manly courage" as
soon as He needs it. If we apply this lesson to ourselves,
More assures us that

> so too each of our angels will bring us from His Spirit
> consolation that will give us the strength to persevere in
> those deeds that will lift us up to heaven. And in order to
> make us completely confident of this fact, Christ went
> there before us by the same method, by the same path.
> For after He had suffered this agony for a long time, His
> spirits were so restored that He arose, returned to His
> apostles, and freely went out to meet the traitor and the
> tormentors who were seeking Him to make Him suffer.
> (45)

Such is Thomas More's advice in his last work, written
during his own final agony. The legendary courage, seren-
ity, and even humor he showed in the midst of his many
final sufferings were rooted in the advice he gives others in
this last testament: "In our agony, remember... His" (45).

Synopsis

The Sadness of Christ is divided into the following general sections:

(1) An introduction (that many may want to skip on
their first reading) giving More's method of scriptural exe-
gesis and a reminder of the alternative each person faces:
Judas or Christ (1-6).

(2) A section that presents the central problem of the

work: what makes Christ "sad unto death"? (Mt 26:38). Although it takes More a while to lay the foundation for his answer, patient readers who "scrutinize carefully enough all the facets of this problem" will discover the basis of his legendary courage (6-17).

(3) A profound explanation of prayer, marked by More's characteristic humor and wit (17-25).

(4) A close analysis of how Christ treats those loved ones who repeatedly fall asleep during His hour of greatest need (25-65).

(5) An analysis of how Christ "as a most conscientious physician" treats Judas the traitor (65-84).

(6) A section entitled "The Severing of Malchus' Ear," marking what More presents as the actual beginning of the Passion. No longer sad or fearful, Christ acts decisively, "rendering good for evil" (85-103).

(7) "The Flight of the Disciples," which points to the importance and difficulty of patience and detachment (104-114).

(8) The brief "Capture of Christ," in which More indicates that Christ is taken only after He has accomplished all that His Father willed (112-114).

(9) Finally, a collection of scriptural quotations and brief commentaries that More wrote out, probably for his meditation in preparation for writing this work (115-127).

Final Prayers and Instructions

Also included in this book are the three final prayers and two instructions which More wrote while in the Tower of London awaiting trial and execution. The first prayer is "The Invocation of Divine Help Against Temptation," a collection of passages from the Psalms. We do not know if More actually wrote out this final version, but we have his psalter in which he marked these passages and made marginal notations. These notations are included in brackets within the text.

His instruction on "How to Treat Those Who Wrong Us" gives strong reasons why one should "bear no malice or evil will to anyone living." It and the instruction "On Saving One's Life" reveal an attitude that was strikingly present throughout the end of More's life. This sentiment recurs frequently in his letters and is perhaps best articulated in the last words he spoke on the scaffold: "I die the King's good servant, but God's first."

This attitude of good will also permeates the "Meditation on Detachment," a prayer More wrote in the margins of his prayer book. Here he asks for such detachment that he might "think my worst enemies my best friends." After all, he reasons, calling to mind the famous story in Genesis, "the brethren of Joseph could never have done him so much good with their love and favor as they did him with their malice and hatred."

Finally, this same attitude shines forth in his "Prayer in Preparation for Death." Written after his trial, shortly before his execution, this prayer begins with an invocation to the Trinity, an examination of conscience from the time of his childhood, and prayers for true repentance. After calling to mind the "wonderful agony" studied in *The Sadness of Christ*, he sets forth a series of prayers that culminates in an ardent spiritual communion, followed by prayers for mercy and concluded with prayers for his friends and enemies. Clearly intending this prayer for others besides himself, More expresses with the last strokes of his pen what he devoted all his life to carrying out: "The things, good Lord, that I pray for, give me the grace to labor for. Amen."

In these final selections I have occasionally taken liberty in rendering More's sixteenth-century English into a modern-day idiom. Those who wish can find the original in volume 13 of *The Complete Works of St. Thomas More*, edited by Garry Haupt. Ardent followers of this saint will also wish to enjoy volume 14, a great work of scholarship which gives More's original manuscript with his corrections, along with Latin transcription and English translation on facing pages. In a separate volume of notes, Clarence Miller gives a brilliant assessment of both style and theme. I am grateful to Dr. Miller and to Yale University Press for the use of his fine translation of *De Tristitia Christi* and to Mary Gottschalk for her help in preparing this edition.

About Sir Thomas More

Thomas More rose from humble origins to achieve the highest political and judicial office of England, second only to that of the king. He was recognized throughout early sixteenth-century Europe as one of the great lawyers, Christian humanists, and classical scholars of his day. Even at a very early age, More gave clear evidence of his uncommon gifts. Because of this, a family friend successfully persuaded his father to allow him to attend Oxford University. More so enjoyed his studies there that his father became alarmed. Two years into the program, he decided that his son should learn something useful. Under what seems to have been considerable coercion, Thomas returned to London to study law at New Inn. Although this law program was among the best and most demanding in London, More found time to continue his study of Greek, philosophy, literature, and theology with such world-renowned teachers as Linacre, Grocyn, and Colet, as well as with the pious and learned Carthusians.

Meanwhile, More excelled at his legal studies at the New Inn. Once finished, he read through the law again at Lincoln's Inn for two more years, after which he was chosen as reader at Furnivall's Inn and reappointed for three successive years — a considerable honor for such a young man. During these years of studying and teaching, More continued an intense life of prayer, during which time he sought to discern his vocation in life. By the age of 25, More was convinced that his place was with city and family, not monastery and cell. At 26 he was elected to Parliament; at 27 he married Jane Colt and fathered four children in the next five years. Jane died when More was 33, leaving him with four young children during the height of his career as a lawyer. Despite his deep sorrow, he married again within one month for the sake of his children. He married the best woman he knew, Alice Middleton, who had neither his interests nor his playful temperament and who was six or seven years his senior. As Erasmus recounts, she was "neither a pearl nor a girl . . . but a shrewd and careful housewife." He marvels that More's "life with her is as pleasant and agreeable as if she had all the charm of youth, and with his buoyant gaiety he wins her to more compliance than he could by severity."

With his gifts of intellectual genius and endearing wit plus his reputation for virtue, More was much sought after as a lawyer and diplomat. He was chosen, for example, by the London merchants to represent them on three major embassies to foreign countries. At the age.of 32, he began his work as a judge, a position that made him well-known and loved among the general London citizenry. Throughout these years, More was also active in the areas of literature and philosophy. The *Utopia*, a work considered by some to be one of the finest Socratic dialogues of all time, has long been recognized as his masterpiece. After fifteen years of prosperous civic life, More was called to serve the King at court, a position he did not and would not seek out. Early on, he was well aware of the dangers of political life; he valued his freedom for family and writing, and he knew that giving up his lucrative law practice to enter public service would cost him a considerable portion of his income. Yet as a loyal citizen, More considered it the "duty of every good man" to contribute to the service of his country. Once in the King's service, More commanded Henry VIII's friendship and trust, serving primarily as his personal secretary, but with some administrative and diplomatic responsibilities. He rose steadily over the next ten years, finally becoming Chancellor in 1529, at the age of fifty-one. As Chancellor, More concentrated on two major tasks: (1) streamlining and improving the judicial system; (2) addressing and personally refuting errors which he considered seditious and destructive of both state and church. In fulfilling this latter task, he collected evidence which resulted in the execution of three persons. Although these executions have captured the imagination of many scholars today, More spent most of his working hours trying to fulfill his function as chief justice of the land. In the assessment of Tudor historian John Guy, More made substantial contributions in this area, reforming the legal system far more effectively than Cromwell would later, in his far-reaching legislative reforms of the 1530s.

More was Chancellor for only thirty-one months. He resigned on May 16, 1532, the day after Henry VIII and Cromwell manipulated the Parliament to take away the traditional freedom of the Church, a freedom that had been written into English law since the Magna Carta. At issue was the survival of the Church as well as the nature of law and the scope of the state's legitimate authority.

Imprisoned in the Tower of London for fifteen months before his execution, More was heavily pressured by his family and friends to sign the oath accepting Henry VIII as the Supreme Head of the Church in England. More steadfastly refused but never expressed animosity towards those who complied. During this time, he wrote a number of devotional and exegetical works, including *A Dialogue of Comfort Against Tribulation, A Treatise on the Passion,* and *The Sadness of Christ.*

That More was God's servant first and foremost was readily seen in his life of prayer and penance. From the time he was a young man, More started each day with private prayer, spiritual reading, and Mass, regardless of his many duties. He lived demanding mortifications in his characteristically discreet and merry manner. He generously cared for the poor and needy, and involved his own children in this same work. He had special devotion to the Blessed Sacrament, to frequent meditation on the Passion, and to the rosary. More was executed on July 6, 1535, and canonized on May 19, 1935. He has become a symbol of professional integrity, famous for the balanced judgment, ever-present humor, and undaunted courage that led him to be known, even in his own lifetime, as the "man for all seasons."

Gerard Wegemer
December 12, 1992

For additional information about St. Thomas More:

Bolt, Robert. *A Man for All Seasons: A Play in Two Acts.* NY: Random House, 1960. (Do not miss the movie version of this play, starring Paul Scofield, directed by Fred Zinnemann, and winner of six academy awards in 1966.)

Chambers, Raymond W. *Thomas More.* London: Jonathan Cape, 1935.

Guy, J. A. *The Public Career of Sir Thomas More.* Yale University Press, 1980.

Martz, Louis L. *Thomas More: Search for the Inner Man.* Yale University Press, 1990.

Maynard, Theodore. *Humanist as Hero.* NY: Macmillan, 1947.

More, Thomas. *The Complete Works of St. Thomas More.* Yale University Press, 1963- .

——————. *Selected Letters.* Tr. Elizabeth Rogers. Princeton University Press, 1947.

Reynolds, E. E. *The Field Is Won.* Burns and Oates, 1968.

Roper, William. *Lives of Sir Thomas More.* NY: Everyman's Library, 1963.

Stapleton, Thomas. *The Life and Illustrious Martyrdom of Sir Thomas More.* NY: Fordham University Press, 1984.

The Sadness, the Weariness, the Fear and the Prayer of Christ Before He Was Taken Prisoner

A Commentary on Matthew 26, Mark 14, Luke 22, John 18.

When Jesus had said these things, they recited the hymn and went out to the Mount of Olives. [Mt 26:30]
Though He had spoken at length about holiness during the supper with His apostles, nevertheless He finished His discourses with a hymn when He was ready to leave. Alas, how different we are from Christ, though we call ourselves Christians: our conversation during meals is not only meaningless and inconsequential (and even for such negligence Christ warned us that we will have to render an accounting), but often our table-talk is also vicious; and then finally, when we are bloated with food and drink, we leave the table without giving thanks to God for the banquets He has bestowed upon us, with never a thought for the gratitude we owe Him.

Paul of Saint Mary, Archbishop of Burgos, a learned, holy man and an outstanding investigator of sacred subjects, gives some convincing arguments to show that the hymn which Christ at that time recited with His apostles consisted of those six psalms which, taken together, are called by the Jews "The Great Alleluia"—namely, Psalm 113 and the five following it. For from very ancient times the Jews have followed the custom of reciting these six psalms, under the name "Great Alleluia," as a prayer of thanksgiving at the Passover and certain other principal

1

feasts, and even now they still go through the same hymn on the same feast days.

But as for us, though we used to say different hymns of thanksgiving and benediction at meals according to the different times of the year, each hymn suited to its season, we have now permitted almost all of them to fall out of use, and we rest content with saying two or three words, no matter what, before going away; and even those few words we mumble merely for form's sake, muttering through our yawns.

"They went out to the Mount of Olives," not to bed. The prophet says, "I arose in the middle of the night to pay homage to you" [Ps 119:62], but Christ did not even lie down in bed. But as for us, I wish we could truly apply to ourselves even this text: "I thought of you as I lay in my bed" [Ps 63:6].

Moreover, it was not yet summer when Christ left the supper and went over to the mount. For it was not that much beyond the vernal equinox, and that the night was cold is clearly shown by the fact that the servants were warming themselves around charcoal fires in the courtyard of the high priest. But this was not the first time that Christ had done this, as the evangelist clearly testifies when he says, "... as He customarily did" [Lk 22:39]. He went up a mountain to pray, teaching us by this sign that when we prepare ourselves to pray, we must lift up our minds from the bustling confusion of human concerns to the contemplation of heavenly things.

Mount Olivet itself also has a mysterious significance, planted as it was with olive trees. For the olive branch was generally used as a symbol of peace, which Christ came to establish between God and man after their long alienation. Moreover, the oil which is produced from the olive represents the anointing by the Spirit, for Christ came and then returned to His Father in order to send the Holy Spirit upon the disciples, so that His anointing might then teach them what they would not have been able to bear had it been told them only a short time before.

Across the stream Cedron to the outlying estate named Gethsemane. [Jn 18:1, Mt 26:36, Mk 14:32]
The stream Cedron lies between the city of Jerusalem and the Mount of Olives, and the word "Cedron" in Hebrew means "sadness." The name "Gethsemane" in Hebrew means "most fertile valley" or "valley of olives." And so there is no reason for us to attribute it merely to chance that the evangelists recorded these place-names so carefully. For if that were the case, once they had reported that He went to the Mount of Olives they would have considered that they had said quite enough, if it were not that God had veiled under these place-names some mysterious meanings which attentive men, with the help of the Holy Spirit, would try to uncover because the names were mentioned. And so, since not a single syllable can be thought inconsequential in a composition which was dictated by the Holy Spirit as the apostles wrote it, and since not a sparrow falls to the earth without God's direction, I cannot think either that the evangelists mentioned those names accidentally or that the Jews assigned them to the places (whatever they themselves intended when they named them) without a secret plan (though unknown to the Jews themselves) of the Holy Spirit, who concealed in these names a store of sacred mysteries to be ferreted out sometime later.

But since "Cedron" means "sadness" and also "blackness," and since this same word is the name not only of the stream mentioned by the evangelists but also (as is sufficiently established) of the valley through which the stream flows and which separates the city from the estate Gethsemane, these names (if their effect is not blocked by our drowsiness) remind us that while we are exiled from the Lord (as the apostle says [2 Cor 5:6]), we must surely cross over, before we come to the fruitful Mount of Olives and the pleasant estate of Gethsemane—an estate which is not gloomy and ugly to look at but most fertile in every sort of joy—we must (I say) cross over the valley and stream of Cedron, a valley of tears and a stream of sadness whose waves can wash away the blackness and filth of our sins. But if we get so weary of pain and grief that we perversely attempt to change this world, this place of labor and penance, into a joyful haven of rest, if we seek heaven on earth, we cut ourselves off forever from true happiness and will drown ourselves in penance when it is too late to do any good and in unbearable, unending tribulations as well.

This, then, is the very salutary lesson contained in these place-names, so fittingly chosen are they. But as the words of holy Scripture are not tied to one sense only but rather are teeming with various mysterious meanings, these place-names harmonize with the immediate context of Christ's passion very well, as if for that reason alone God's eternal providence had seen to it that these places should long beforehand have been designated by such names as would prove to be, some centuries later, preordained tokens of His passion, as the comparison of His deeds with the names would show. For since "Cedron" means "blackened," does it not seem to recall that prediction of the prophet that Christ would work out His glory by means of inglorious torment, that He would be disfigured by dark bruises, gore, spittle, and dirt? "There is nothing beautiful or handsome about his face" [Is 53:2].

Then, too, the meaning of the stream He crossed— "sad"—was far from irrelevant, as He Himself testified when He said, "My soul is sad unto death."

And His disciples also followed Him. [Lk 22:39]
That is, the eleven who had remained followed Him.
As for the twelfth, the devil entered into him after the
morsel and made off with him, so that he did not follow
the master as a disciple but pursued Him as a traitor and
bore out only too well what Christ said: "He who is not
with me is against me." Against Christ he certainly was,
since at that very moment he was preparing to spring his
trap for Him, while the other disciples were following
after Him to pray. Let us follow after Christ and pray to
the Father together with Him. Let us not emulate Judas
by departing from Christ after partaking of His favors
and dining excellently with Him, lest we should bear out
that prophecy, "If you saw a thief you ran away with
him" [Ps 50:18].

*Judas, who betrayed Him, also knew the place, because
Jesus frequently went there with His disciples. [Jn 18:2]*
Once again the evangelists take advantage of mentioning the betrayer to emphasize for us, and to recommend to
us by such emphasis, Christ's holy custom of going
together with His disciples to that place in order to pray.
For if He had gone there only on some nights and not frequently, the betrayer would not have been so completely
convinced he would find our Lord there that he could
afford to bring the servants of the high priest and a Roman
cohort there as if everything had been definitely arranged;
for if they had found that it was not arranged, they would
have thought he was playing a practical joke on them and
would not have let him get away with it unscathed. Now
where are those people who think they are men of stature,
who are proud of themselves as if they had done something fine, if sometimes on the vigil of a special feast they
either continue their prayers a little longer into the night
or get up earlier for their morning prayers? Our Savior

Christ had the habit of spending whole nights without sleep in order to pray.

Where are those who called Him a glutton for food and wine because He did not refuse to go to the banquets of the publicans and did not think it beneath Him to attend the celebrations of sinful men? Where are those who thought that by comparison with the strict regimen of the Pharisees His morals were hardly better than those of the common rabble? But while these gloomy hypocrites were praying on the corners of the main thoroughfares so that they might be seen by men, He was eating lunch with sinners, calmly and kindly helping them to reform their lives. On the other hand, He used to spend the night praying under the open sky while the hypocritical Pharisee was snoring away in his soft bed. How I wish that those of us who are prevented by our own laziness from imitating the illustrious example of our Savior might at least be willing to call to mind His all-night vigils when we turn over on the other side in our beds, half asleep, and that we might then, during the short time before we fall asleep again, offer Him thanks, condemn our slothfulness, and pray for an increase of grace. Surely if we set out to make a habit of doing even the least little bit of good, I feel certain that God will soon set us forward a great way on the path of virtue.

And He said, "Sit down here while I go over there to pray." And He took Peter and the two sons of Zebedee with Him. He began to feel sorrow and grief and fear and weariness. Then He said to them, "My soul is sad unto death. Stay here and keep watch with me." [Mt 26:36-38, Mk 14:32-34]

Commanding the other eight to stop somewhat lower down, He went further on, taking with Him Peter, John, and his brother James, the three whom He had always singled out from the rest of the apostles by a certain special

privilege of intimacy. Now even if He had done this for no
other reason than that He wanted to, no one ought to have
been envious because of His generosity. But still there were
certain reasons for this which He might well have had in
mind. For Peter was outstanding for his zealous faith and
John for his virginity, and his brother James was to be the
very first of all to suffer martyrdom in the name of Christ.
Furthermore, these were the three to whom He had formerly granted the secret knowledge and open sight of His
glorified body. It was only right, then, that those same
three whom He had admitted to such an extraordinary
vision, and whom He had invigorated with a momentary
flash of the eternal brilliance so that they ought to have
been stronger than the others, should have assigned to
them the role of His nearest supporters in the preliminary
agony of His passion. But when He had gone on a little
way, He suddenly felt such a sharp and bitter attack of
sadness, grief, fear, and weariness that He immediately
uttered, even in their presence, those anguished words
which gave expression to His overburdened feelings: "My
soul is sad unto death."

For a huge mass of troubles took possession of the tender and gentle body of our most holy Savior. He knew that
His ordeal was now imminent and just about to overtake
Him: the treacherous betrayer, the bitter enemies, binding
ropes, false accusations, slanders, blows, thorns, nails, the
cross, and horrible tortures stretched out over many hours.
Over and above these, He was tormented by the thought of
His disciples' terror, the loss of the Jews, even the destruction of the very man who so disloyally betrayed Him, and
finally the ineffable grief of His beloved mother. The gathered storm of all these evils rushed into His most gentle
heart and flooded it like the ocean sweeping through broken dikes.

Perhaps someone may wonder how it could be that our Savior Christ could feel sadness, sorrow, and grief, since He was truly God, equal to His all-powerful Father. Certainly He could not have felt them if He had been God (as He was) in such a way as not to be man also. But as a matter of fact, since He was no less really a man than He was really God, I see no reason for us to be surprised that insofar as He was man, He had the ordinary feelings of mankind (though certainly no blameworthy ones)—no more than we would be surprised that insofar as He was God, He performed stupendous miracles. For if we are surprised that Christ felt fear, weariness, and grief, simply on the grounds that He was God, why should we not also be surprised that He experienced hunger, thirst, and sleep, seeing that He was none the less divine for doing these things? But here, perhaps, you may object, "I am no longer surprised at His capacity for these emotions, but I cannot help being surprised at His desire to experience them. For He taught His disciples not to be afraid of those who can kill the body only and can do nothing beyond that; and how can it be fitting that He Himself should now be very much afraid of those same persons, especially since even His body could suffer nothing from them except what He Himself allowed?

"Furthermore, since we know His martyrs rushed to their deaths eagerly and joyfully, triumphing over tyrants and torturers, how can it not seem inappropriate that Christ Himself, the very prototype and leader of martyrs, the standard-bearer of them all, should be so terrified at the approach of pain, so shaken, so utterly downcast? Shouldn't He rather have been especially careful to set a good example in this matter, just as He had always let His deeds precede His precepts, so that others might learn from His own example to undergo death eagerly for truth's sake and so that those who afterwards would suffer death for the faith with fear and hesitation might not indulge their slackness by imagining that they are following Christ's precedent?—whereas actually their reluctance would both detract a great deal from the glory of their cause and discourage others who observe their sadness and fear." Those who bring up these objections and others of the same sort do not scrutinize carefully enough all the facets of this problem and do not pay enough attention to what Christ meant when He forbade His followers to fear death. For He hardly intended it to mean that they should never under any circumstances recoil from a violent death, but rather that they should not, out of fear, flee from a death which will not last, only to run, by denying the faith, into one which will be everlasting. For He wished His followers to be brave and prudent soldiers, not senseless and foolish. The brave man bears up under the blows which beset him; the senseless man simply does not feel them when they strike. Only a foolish man does not fear wounds, but a prudent man does not allow any fear of suffering to divert him from a holy way of life, for that would be to refuse lesser pains at the expense of plunging himself into far more bitter ones.

When an afflicted part of the body is to be cut or cauterized, the doctor does not try to persuade the sick man not to feel any mental anguish at the thought of the pain the cutting or burning will cause, but rather encourages him to bear up under it. He admits it will be painful, but stresses that the pain will be outweighed by the pleasure of health and the avoidance of even more horrible pain. Indeed, though our Savior Christ commands us to suffer death (when it cannot be avoided) rather than fall away from Him through a fear of death (and we do fall away from Him when we publicly deny our faith in Him), still He is so far from requiring us to do violence to our nature by not fearing death at all that He even leaves us free to flee from punishment (whenever this can be done without injury to His cause). "If you are persecuted in one city," He says, "flee to another" [Mt 10:23]. This permission, this cautious advice of a prudent master, was followed by almost all the apostles and by almost all the illustrious martyrs in the many succeeding centuries: there is hardly one of them who did not use it at some time or other to save his life and extend it, with great profit to himself and others, until such a time as the hidden providence of God foresaw was more fitting.

On the other hand, some brave champions have taken the initiative by publicly professing their Christianity, though no one was trying to discover it, and by freely exposing themselves to death, though no one was demanding it. Thus God chose, according to His pleasure, to increase His glory sometimes by concealing the riches of the faith, so that those who set clever traps for His believers might be duped, sometimes by displaying them, so that those who cruelly persecuted His followers might be incensed by seeing all their hopes frustrated and finding, much to their outrage, that all their ferocity could not overcome martyrs who met death willingly. But God in His mercy does not command us to climb this steep and lofty peak of bravery, and hence it is not safe for just anyone to go rushing on heedlessly to the point where he cannot retrace his steps gradually but may be in danger of falling head over heels into the abyss if he cannot make it to the summit. As for those whom God calls to do this, let them choose their goal and pursue it successfully and they will reign in triumph. He keeps hidden the times, the moments, the causes of all things, and when the time is right He brings forth all things from the secret treasure-chest of His wisdom, which penetrates all things irresistibly and disposes all things sweetly [Ws 8:1].

And so if anyone is brought to the point where he

must either suffer torment or deny God, he need not doubt that it was God's will for him to be brought to this crisis. Therefore he has very good reason to hope for the best. For God will either extricate him from the struggle or else He will aid him in the fight and make him conquer so that He may crown him with the conqueror's wreath. "For God is trustworthy," the apostle says. "He does not allow you to be tempted beyond what you can stand, but with the temptation He also gives a way out so that you may be able to bear it" [1 Cor 10:13]. Therefore, when things have come to the point of a hand-to-hand combat with the prince of this world, the devil, and his cruel underlings, and there is no way left to withdraw without disgracing the cause, then I would think that a man ought to cast away fear and I would direct him to be completely calm, confident, and hopeful. "For," says the Scripture, "whoever lacks confidence on the day of tribulation, his courage will be lessened" [Prov 24:10].

But before the actual engagement, fear is not reprehensible as long as reason does not cease to struggle against fear—a struggle which is not criminal or sinful but rather an immense opportunity for merit. For do you imagine that since those most holy martyrs shed their blood for the faith, they had no fear at all of death and torments? On this point I will not pause to draw up a list; to me Paul may stand for a thousand others. Indeed, if David was worth ten thousand soldiers in the war against the Philistines, then certainly Paul can also be considered worth ten thousand soldiers in the battle for the faith against faithless persecutors. And so this bravest of champions Paul, who was so far advanced in hope and the love of Christ that he had no doubts about his heavenly reward, who said, "I have fought the good fight, I have finished the race, and now there remains for me a crown of justice" [2 Tm 4:7-8], which he longed for so ardently that he said, "For me to live is Christ and to die is gain" and "I long to be dissolved and to be with Christ" [Phil 1:21, 23]—nevertheless this very same Paul not only managed skillfully to escape from the snares of the Jews by means of the tribune [Acts 23:6-35] but also freed himself from prison by declaring that he was a Roman citizen [Acts 22:25-29], and once again he eluded the cruelty of the Jews by appealing to Caesar [Acts 25:10-12], and he escaped the hands of the impious King Aretas by being let down from the wall in a basket [2 Cor 11:32-33].

But if anyone should contend that he was looking to the fruit that was to be planted afterwards through his efforts, and that throughout these events he was not frightened by any fear of death, certainly I will freely grant the first point, but I would not venture to assert the second. For that most brave heart of the apostle was not impervious to fear, as he himself clearly shows when he writes to the Corinthians, "For even when we came to Macedonia, our flesh had no rest but suffered all manner of affliction, conflicts without, fears within" [2 Cor 7:5]. And in another place he wrote to the same persons, "I was with you in weakness and fear and much trembling" [1 Cor 2:3]. And once again, "For we do not wish you, brethren, to be ignorant of the affliction which came upon us in Asia, since we were burdened beyond measure, beyond our strength, so that we were weary even of life" [2 Cor 1:8]. In these passages do you not hear from Paul's own mouth his fear, his trembling, his weariness more unbearable than death itself, so that his experience seems to call to mind that agony of Christ and to present, as it were, an image of it? Go ahead now and deny if you can that Christ's holy martyrs felt fear at the terrible prospect of death. But on the other hand, no amount of terror, however great, could deter this same Paul from his program of advancing the faith, and no advice from the disciples could persuade him not to go to Jerusalem (to which he felt he was called by the Spirit of God), even though the prophet Agabus had foretold that chains and certain dangers were awaiting him there [Acts 21:10-13].

And so the fear of death and torments carries no stigma of guilt but rather is an affliction of the sort Christ came to suffer, not to escape. We should not immediately consider it cowardice for someone to feel fear and horror at the thought of torments, not even if he prudently avoids dangers (provided he does not compromise himself); but to flee because of a fear of torture and death when the circumstances make it necessary to fight, or to give up all hope of victory and surrender to the enemy, that, to be sure, is a capital crime according to the [Justinian] military code. But otherwise, no matter how much the heart of the soldier is agitated and stricken by fear, if he still comes forward at the command of the general, goes on, fights, and defeats the enemy, he has no reason to fear that his former fear might lessen his reward in any way. As a matter of fact, he ought to receive even more praise because of it, since he had to overcome not only the enemy but also his own fear, which is often harder to conquer than the enemy himself.

As for our Savior Christ, what happened a little later showed how far He was from letting His sadness, fear, and weariness prevent Him from obeying His Father's command and keep Him from carrying out with courage all those things which He had formerly regarded with a wise and wholesome fear. For the time being, however, He had more than one reason why He should choose to suffer fear, sadness, weariness, and grief—"choose," I say, not "be forced," for who could have forced God? Quite the contrary, it was by His own marvelous arrangement that His divinity moderated its influence on His humanity for such a time and in such a way that He was able to yield to the passions of our frail humanity and to suffer them with such terrible intensity. But as I was saying, Christ, in His wonderful generosity, chose to do this for a number of reasons. First of all, in order to do that for which He came into the world—that is, to bear witness to the truth. And then, although He was truly man and also truly God, still there have been some who, seeing the truth of His human nature in His hunger, thirst, sleep, weariness, and suchlike, have falsely persuaded themselves that He was not true God—I do not mean the Jews and gentiles of His time who rejected Him, but rather the people of a much later time who even professed His name and His faith, namely, heretics like Arius and his followers, who denied that Christ was of one nature with the Father and thus embroiled the Church in great strife for many years. But against such plagues as this Christ provided a very powerful antidote, the endless supply of His miracles.

But there also arose an equal danger on the other side, just as those who escaped Scylla had to cope with Charybdis. For there were some who fixed their gaze so intently on the glory of His signs and powers that they were stunned and dazed by that immense brightness and went so far wrong as to deny altogether that He was truly a man. These people too, growing from their original founder into a sect, did not hesitate to rend the holy unity of the Catholic Church and to tear it apart with their disgraceful sedition. This insane belief of theirs, which is no less dangerous than it is false, seeks to undermine and subvert completely (so far as lies within their power) the mystery of mankind's redemption, since it strives to utterly cut off and dry up the spring (as it were) from which the stream of our salvation flowed forth, namely, the death and passion of our Savior. And so, to cure this very deadly disease, the best and kindest of physicians chose to experience sadness, dread, weariness, and fear of tortures and thus to show by these very real signs of human frailty that

He was really a man.

Moreover, because He came into the world to earn joy for us by His own sorrow, and since that future joy of ours was to be fulfilled in our souls as well as our bodies, so too He chose to experience not only the pain of torture in His body but also the most bitter feelings of sadness, fear, and weariness in His mind, partly in order to bind us to Him all the more by reason of His greater sufferings for us, partly in order to admonish us how wrong it is for us either to refuse to suffer grief for His sake (since He freely bore so many and such immense griefs for us) or to tolerate grudgingly the punishment due to our sins, since we see our holy Savior Himself endured by His own free choice such numerous and bitter kinds of torment, both bodily and mental—and that not because He deserved them through any fault of His own, but rather in order to do away with the wicked deeds which we alone committed.

Finally, since nothing was hidden from His eternal foreknowledge, He foresaw that there would be people of various temperaments in the Church (which is His own mystical body)—that His members (I say) would differ considerably in their makeup. And although nature alone, without the help of grace, is quite incapable of enduring martyrdom (since, as the apostle says, "no one can say 'Jesus is Lord' except in the Spirit" [1 Cor 12:3]), nevertheless God does not impart grace to men in such a way as to suspend for the moment the functions and duties of nature, but instead He either allows nature to accommodate itself to the grace which is superadded to it, so that the good deed may be performed with all the more ease, or else, if nature is disposed to resist, so that this very resistance, overcome and put down by grace, may add to the merit of the deed because it was difficult to do.

Therefore, since He foresaw that there would be many people of such a delicate constitution that they would be convulsed with terror at any danger of being tortured, He chose to enhearten them by the example of His own sorrow, His own sadness, His own weariness and unequalled fear, lest they should be so disheartened as they compare their own fearful state of mind with the boldness of the bravest martyrs that they would yield freely what they fear will be won from them by force. To such a person as this, Christ wanted His own deed to speak out (as it were) with His own living voice: "O faint of heart, take courage and do not despair. You are afraid, you are sad, you are stricken with weariness and dread of the torment with which you have been cruelly threatened. Trust me. I conquered the world, and yet I suffered immeasurably more from fear, I was sadder, more afflicted with weariness, more horrified at the prospect of such cruel suffering drawing eagerly nearer and nearer. Let the brave man have his high-spirited martyrs, let him rejoice in imitating a thousand of them. But you, my timorous and feeble little sheep, be content to have me alone as your shepherd, follow my leadership; if you do not trust yourself, place your trust in me. See, I am walking ahead of you along this fearful road. Take hold of the border of my garment and you will feel going out from it a power which will stay your heart's blood from issuing in vain fears and will make your mind more cheerful, especially when you remember that you are following closely in my footsteps (and I am to be trusted and will not allow you to be tempted beyond what you can bear, but I will give together with the temptation a way out that you may be able to endure it), and likewise when you remember that this light and momentary burden of tribulation will prepare for you a weight of glory which is beyond all measure. For the sufferings of this time are not worthy to be compared with the glory to come which will be revealed in you. As you reflect on such things, take heart and use the sign of my cross to drive away this dread, this sadness, fear, and weariness like vain specters of the darkness. Advance successfully and press through all obstacles, firmly confident that I will champion your cause until you are victorious and then in turn will reward you with the laurel crown of victory."

And so among the other reasons why our Savior deigned to take upon Himself these feelings of human weakness, this one I have spoken of is not unworthy of consideration—I mean that having made Himself weak for the sake of the weak, He might take care of other weak men by means of His own weakness. He had their welfare so much at heart that this whole process of His agony seems designed for nothing more clearly than to lay down a fighting technique and a battle code for the fainthearted soldier who needs to be swept along, as it were, into martyrdom.

For in order to teach anyone assailed by a fear of imminent danger that he should both ask others to watch and pray and still place his trust in God alone apart from the others, and likewise in order to signify that He would tread the bitter winepress of His cross alone without any companion [Is 63:3], He commanded those same three apostles whom He had chosen from the other eight and taken on with Him almost to the foot of the mount, to stop there and to bear up and watch with Him; but He Himself withdrew from them about a stone's throw.

And going on a little way, He fell face down on the earth and prayed that if it were possible, the hour might pass from Him. And He said: "Abba, Father, to you all things are possible. Take this cup away from me; but yet not what I will, but what you will. My Father, if it is possible, let this cup pass away from me; yet not as I will, but as you will." [Mt 26:39, Mk 14:35-36]

First of all, Christ the commander teaches by His own example that His soldier should take humility as his starting point, since it is the foundation (as it were) of all the virtues from which one may safely mount to higher levels. For though His divinity is equal and identical to that of God the Father, nevertheless because He is also man He casts Himself down humbly as a man, face down on the earth before God the Father.

Reader, let us pause for a little at this point and contemplate with a devout mind our commander lying on the ground in humble supplication. For if we do this carefully, a ray of that light which enlightens every man who comes into the world will illuminate our minds so that we will see, recognize, deplore, and at long last correct, I will not say the negligence, sloth, or apathy, but rather the feeblemindedness, the insanity, the downright blockheaded stupidity with which most of us approach the all-powerful God and instead of praying reverently, address Him in a lazy and sleepy sort of way; and by the same token I am very much afraid that instead of placating Him and gaining His favor we exasperate Him and sharply provoke His wrath.

I wish that sometime we would make a special effort, right after finishing our prayers, to run over in our minds the whole sequence of time we spent praying. What follies will we see there? How much absurdity and sometimes even foulness will we catch sight of? Indeed, we will be amazed that it was at all possible for our minds to dissipate themselves in such a short time among so many places at such great distance from each other, among so many different affairs, such various, such manifold, such idle pursuits. For if someone, just as an experiment, should make a determined effort to make his mind touch upon as many and as diverse objects as possible, I hardly think that in such a short time he could run through such disparate and numerous topics as the mind, left to its own devices, ranges through while the mouth negligently

mumbles through the hours of the office and other much-
used prayers.

And so if anyone wonders or has any doubts about
what the mind is doing while dreams take over our consciousness during sleep, I find no comparison that comes
closer to the mark than to think that the mind is occupied
during sleep in exactly the same way as are the minds of
those who are awake (if those who pray in this way can be
said to be awake) but whose thoughts wander wildly during prayers, frantically flitting about in a throng of absurd
fantasies—with this difference, though, from the sleeping
dreamer: some of the waking dreamer's strange sights
which his mind embraces in its foreign travels while his
tongue runs rattling through his prayers as if they were
mere sound without sense, some of these strange sights
are such filthy and abominable monstrosities that if they
had been seen during sleep, certainly no one, no matter
how shameless, would have the nerve to recount such
extravagant dreams after he woke up, not even in the
company of stable-boys.

And undoubtedly that old saying is very true, that our
looks are a mirror of our minds. For certainly such a wild
and deranged state of mind is distinctly reflected in the
eyes, in the cheeks, eyelids, and eyebrows, in the hands,
feet, and, in short, in the overall bearing of the entire body.
For just as our minds are inattentive when we set out to
pray, so too we proceed to do so with an equally careless
and sprawling deportment of our bodies.

True, we do pretend that the worship of God is our
reason for wearing better than everyday clothes on feast
days, but the negligence with which most of us pray makes
it utterly clear that we have utterly failed to conceal the
real motive, namely, a haughty desire to show off in the
eyes of the world. Thus in our negligence we sometimes
stroll around, sometimes sit down on a stool. And even

when we kneel down, we either place our weight on one knee, raising up the other and resting it on our foot, or we place a cushion under our knees, and sometimes (if we are especially spoiled) we even support our elbows on a cushion, looking for all the world like a propped-up house that is threatening to tumble down.

And then our actions too, in how many ways do they betray that our minds are wandering miles away? We scratch our heads, clean our fingernails with a pocketknife, pick our noses with our fingers, meanwhile making the wrong responses. Having no idea what we have already said and what we have not said, we make a wild guess as to what remains to be said. Are we not ashamed to pray in such a deranged state of mind and body—to beseech God's favor in a matter so crucial for us, to beg His forgiveness for so many monstrous misdeeds, to ask Him to save us from eternal punishment?—so that even if we had not sinned before, we would still deserve tenfold eternal torments for having approached the majesty of God in such a contemptuous fashion.

Imagine, if you will, that you have committed a crime of high treason against some mortal prince or other who has your life in his hands but who is so merciful that he is prepared to temper his wrath because of your repentance and humble supplication, and to commute the death sentence into a monetary fine or even to suspend it completely if you give convincing signs of great shame and sorrow. Now when you have been brought into the presence of the prince, go ahead and speak to him carelessly, casually, without the least concern. While he stays in one place and listens attentively, stroll around here and there as you run through your plea. Then when you have had enough of walking up and down, sit down on a chair, or if courtesy seems to require that you condescend to kneel down, first command someone to come and place a cushion beneath your knees, or better yet, to bring a prie-dieu with another cushion to lean your elbows on. Then yawn, stretch, sneeze, spit without giving it a thought, and belch up the fumes of your gluttony. In short, conduct yourself in such a way that he can clearly see from your face, your voice, your gestures, and your whole bodily deportment that while you are addressing him you are thinking about something else. Tell me now, what success could you hope for from such a plea as this?

Certainly we would consider it quite mad to defend ourselves in this way before a mortal prince against a charge that carries the death penalty. And yet such a prince, once he had destroyed our bodies, could do nothing further. And do we think it is reasonable, when we have been caught committing a whole series of far more serious crimes, to beg pardon so contemptuously from the king of all kings, God Himself, who when He has destroyed our bodies has the power to send both body and soul together to hell?

Still I would not wish anyone to construe what I have said as meaning that I forbid anyone to pray while walking or sitting or even lying down. Indeed, I wish that whatever our bodies may be doing, we would at the same time constantly lift up our minds to God (which is the most acceptable form of prayer). For no matter where we may turn our steps, as long as our minds are directed to God we clearly do not turn away from Him who is present everywhere. But just as the prophet who said to God, "I was mindful of you when I lay upon my bed" did not rest content with that but also rose "in the middle of the night to pay homage to the Lord," so too I would require that besides such prayers said while walking, we also occasionally say some prayers for which we prepare our minds more thoughtfully, for which we dispose our bodies more reverently, than we would if we were about to approach all the kings in the whole world sitting together in one place.

But of this much I can assure you: every time I think about this mental wandering, it vexes and plagues my mind.

Nevertheless, some ideas may be suggested to us during our prayers by an evil spirit or may creep into our imaginations through the normal functioning of our senses, and I would not assert that any one of these, not even if it is vile and quite horrible, must be immediately fatal, so long as we resist it and drive it away. But otherwise, if we accept it with pleasure or allow it through negligence to grow in intensity over a long period of time, I have not the slightest doubt that the force of it can become so aggravated as to be fatally destructive to the soul.

Certainly, when I consider the immeasurable glory of God's majesty I am immediately compelled and forced to believe that if even these brief distractions of mind are not crimes punishable by death, it is only because God in His mercy and goodness deigns not to exact death for them, not because the wickedness inherent in their own nature does not deserve death—and for this reason: I simply cannot imagine how such thoughts can gain entrance into the minds of men when they are praying (that is, when they are speaking to God) unless it be through weakness of faith. Otherwise, since our minds do not go wool-gathering while we are addressing a mortal prince about some important matter or even speaking to one of his ministers who might be in a position of some influence with his master, certainly it could never happen that our minds should stray even the least bit while we are praying to God—certainly not, that is, if we believed with a strong and active faith that we are in the presence of God, who not only listens to our words and looks upon our facial features and bodily deportment as outward signs and indications from which our interior state of mind can be gathered, but who also pierces into the most secret and inward recesses of our hearts with a vision more penetrating than the eyes of [the Argonaut] Lynceus and who illuminates everything with the immeasurable brightness of His majesty—it could not happen, I say, if we believed that God is present, God in whose glorious presence all the princes of the world in all their glory must confess (unless they are out of their minds) that they are the merest mites and earth-creeping worms.

Therefore, since our Savior Christ saw that nothing is more profitable than prayer, but since He was also aware that this means of salvation would very often be fruitless because of the negligence of men and the malice of demons—so much so that it would very frequently be perverted into an instrument of destruction—He decided to take this opportunity, on the way to His death, to reinforce His teaching by His words and example and to put the finishing touches on this most necessary point just as He did on the other parts of His teaching.

He wished us to know that we ought to serve God not only in soul but also in body, since He created both, and He wanted us to learn that a reverent attitude of the body, though it takes its origin and character from the soul, increases by a kind of reflex the soul's own reverence and devotion toward God. Hence He presented the most humble mode of subjection and venerated His heavenly Father in a bodily posture which no earthly prince has dared to demand, or even to accept if freely offered, except that drunken and debauched Macedonian [Alexander] and some other barbarians puffed up with success who thought they ought to be venerated as gods.

For when He prayed He did not sit back or stand up or merely kneel down, but rather He threw His whole body face forward and lay prostrate on the ground. Then, in that pitiable posture, He implored His Father's mercy and twice called His Father by name, begging Him that since all things are possible to Him, He might be moved by His prayers to take away the cup of His passion if this could be done, that is, if He had not imposed it on Him by an immutable decree. But He also asked that His own will, as expressed in this prayer, might not be granted if something else seemed better to His Father's will, which is absolutely best.

This passage should not lead you to think that the Son was ignorant of the will of the Father. Rather, because He wanted to instruct men He also wanted to express the feelings of men. By saying the word "Father" twice, He wanted to remind us that all fatherhood proceeds from Him, both in heaven and on earth [Eph 3:15]. Moreover, He also wanted to impress upon us that God the Father is His father in a double sense—namely, by creation, which is a sort of fatherhood (for we come from God, who created us from nothing, more truly than we do from the human father who begot us, since in fact God created beforehand that begetter Himself, and since He created and supplied beforehand all the matter out of which we were begotten), but when Christ acknowledged God as His Father in this sense, He did so as a man; on the other hand, as God, He knows Him as His natural and coeternal Father.

And yet another reason for His calling on His Father twice may not be far from the truth: He intended not only to acknowledge that God the Father is His natural father in heaven but also to signify that He has no other father on earth, since He was conceived by a virgin mother according to the flesh, without any male seed, when the Holy Spirit came upon His mother—the Spirit, I say, both of the Father and of Himself, whose works coexist in identity and cannot be radically distinguished by any human insight.

Moreover, this forceful repetition of His Father's name, since it expresses an intense desire to gain what He asked for, might serve to teach us a very wholesome lesson: that when we pray for something without receiving it we should not give up like King Saul, who, because he did not immediately receive a prophecy from God, resorted to witchcraft and went off to the woman with a spirit, engaging in a practice forbidden by the law and formerly suppressed by his own decree [1 Kgs 28:5-25].

Christ teaches us that we should persevere in our prayers without murmuring at all if we do not obtain what we seek—and for good reason, since we see that the Son of God, our Savior, did not obtain the reprieve from death which He sought from His Father with such urgency but always with the condition (and this is what we ought to imitate most of all) that His will was subject to the will of His Father.

And He went to His disciples and found them sleeping. [Mt 26:40, Mk 14:37, Lk 22:45]

Notice here how much greater one love is than another. Notice how Christ's love for His own was much greater than the love they gave Him in return, even those who loved Him most. For even the sadness, fear, dread, and weariness which so grievously assailed Him as His most cruel torment drew near could not keep Him from going to see them. But they, on the other hand, however much they loved Him (and undoubtedly they loved Him intensely), even at the very time when such an enormous danger was threatening their loving Master, could still give in to sleep.

And He said to Peter, "Simon, are you sleeping? Could you not stay awake one hour with me? Stay awake and pray that you may not enter into temptation. For the spirit indeed is willing, but the flesh is weak." [Mt 26:40-41, Mk 14:37-38]

This short speech of Christ is remarkably forceful: the

words are mild, but their point is sharp and piercing. For by addressing him as Simon and reproaching him under that name for his sleepiness, Christ tacitly lets it be known that the name Peter, which Christ had previously given him because of his firmness, would hardly be altogether appropriate now, because of this infirmity and sleep. Moreover, not only was the failure to use the name Peter (or rather, Cephas) a barbed omission, but the actual use of the name Simon also carries a sting. For in Hebrew, the language in which Christ was speaking to him, "Simon" means "listening" and also "obedient." But in fact he was neither listening nor obedient, since he went to sleep against Christ's express wishes.

Over and above these, our Savior's gentle words to Peter seem to carry certain other barbed implications, which if He were chiding him more severely would be something like this: "Simon, no longer Cephas, are you sleeping? For how do you deserve to be called Cephas, that is, rock? I singled you out by that name because of your firmness, but now you show yourself to be so infirm that you cannot hold out even for an hour against the inroads of sleep. As for that old name of yours, 'Simon,' certainly you live up to that remarkably well: can you be called listening when you are sleeping this way? Or can you be called obedient when in spite of my instructions to stay awake, I am no sooner gone than you relax and doze and fall asleep? I always made much of you, Simon, and yet, Simon, are you sleeping? I paid you many high honors, and yet, Simon, are you sleeping? A few moments ago you boasted that you would die with me, and now, Simon, are you sleeping? Now I am pursued to the death by the Jews and the gentiles and by one worse than either of them, Judas; and Simon, are you sleeping? Indeed, Satan is busily seeking to sift all of you like wheat, and Simon, are you sleeping? What can I expect from the others, when in such great and pressing danger, not only to me but also to all of you, I find that you, Simon, even you are sleeping?" Then, lest this seem to be a matter which concerned Peter only, He turned and spoke to the others. "Stay awake and pray," He says, "that you may not enter into temptation. The spirit indeed is willing, but the flesh is weak." Here we are enjoined to be constant in prayer, and we are informed that prayer is not only useful but also extremely necessary—for this reason: without it the weakness of the flesh holds us back, somewhat in the way a remora-fish retards a ship, until our minds, no matter how willing to do good, are swept back into the evils of temptation. For whose spirit is more willing than Peter's was? And yet that he had great need of God's protection against the flesh is clear enough from this fact alone: when sleep kept him from praying and begging for God's help, he gave an opening to the devil, who not long afterwards used the weakness of Peter's flesh to blunt the eagerness of his spirit and impelled him to perjure himself by denying Christ. Now if such things happened to the apostles, who were like flourishing green branches, that is, if they entered into temptation when they allowed sleep to interrupt their prayers, what will happen to us, who are like sapless sticks by comparison, if when we are suddenly faced by danger (and when, I ask you, are we not in danger, since our enemy the devil constantly prowls like a roaring lion looking everywhere for someone who is ready to fall because of the weakness of the flesh, ready to pounce upon such a man and devour him)—in such great danger, I say, what will become of us if we do not follow Christ's advice by being steadfast in wakefulness and prayer?

Christ tells us to stay awake, but not for cards and dice, not for rowdy parties and drunken brawls, not for wine and women, but for prayer. He tells us to pray not occasionally but constantly. "Pray," He says, "unceasingly."' He tells us to pray not only during the day (for it is hardly necessary to command anyone to stay awake during the day), but rather He exhorts us to devote to intense prayer a large part of that very time which most of us usually devote entirely to sleep. How much more, then, should we be ashamed of our miserable performance and recognize the enormous guilt we incur by saying no more than a short prayer or two, perhaps, during the day, and even those said as we doze and yawn. Finally our Savior tells us to pray, not that we may roll in wealth, not that we may live in a continuous round of pleasures, not that something awful may happen to our enemies, not that we may receive honor in this world, but rather that we may not enter into temptation. In fact, He wishes us to understand that all those worldly goods are either downright harmful or else, by comparison with that one benefit, the merest trifles; and hence in His wisdom He placed this one petition at the end of the prayer which He had previously taught His disciples, as if it were a summary, in a way, of all the rest: "And lead us not into temptation, but deliver us from evil."

And again He went away, for the second time, and said the same prayer over again in these words: "My Father, if this cup cannot pass away without my drinking it, let your will be done." And He came again and found them sleeping, for their eyes were heavy. And they did not know what answer to make to Him. And leaving them, He went away again and, kneeling down, said the same prayer in these words: "Father, if you are willing, take this cup from me. Yet not my will but yours be done." [Mk 14:39-40, Mt 26:42-44]

Thus after He had given His disciples this warning He went back to pray again, and He repeated the same prayer He had said before, but still in such a way as to commit the whole matter once more to the will of the Father. Thus He teaches us to make our petitions earnest without being absolutely definite, but rather to trust the whole outcome to God, who desires our welfare no less than we ourselves do and who knows what is likely to produce it a thousand times better than we do. "My Father," He says, "if this cup cannot pass away without my drinking it, let your will be done." That pronoun "my" has a twofold effect: for it expresses great affection, and it makes it clear that God the Father is the father of Christ in a singular way—that is, not only by creation (for in this way He is the father of all things), not by adoption (in this way He is the father of Christians), but rather by nature He is God the Father of God the Son. And then He teaches the rest of us to pray thus: "Our Father who art in heaven." By these words we acknowledge that we are all brothers who have one Father in common, whereas Christ Himself is the only one who can rightfully, because of His divinity, address the Father as He does here, "My Father." But if anyone is not content to be like other men and is so proud as to imagine that he alone is governed by the secret Spirit of God and that he has a different status from other men, it certainly seems to me that such a person arrogates to himself the language of Christ and prays with the invocation "My Father" instead of "Our Father," since he claims for himself as a private individual the Spirit which God shares with all men. In fact, such a person is not much different from Lucifer, since he arrogates to himself God's language, just as Lucifer claimed God's place. Christ's language here—"If this cup cannot pass away without my drinking it, let your will be done"—also makes it perfectly clear on what basis He calls a thing possible or impossible, namely, on no other basis than the certain, immutable, unconstrained decision of His Father concerning His death. For otherwise, if He had thought that He was ineluctably and necessarily destined to die, either because of the course of the heavenly bodies or because of some more abstract overall scheme of things such as fate, and if this had been the sense in which He said, "If this cup cannot pass away without my drinking it," then it would have been completely pointless for Him to add the phrase "let your will be done." For how could He have left the matter to be decided by the Father if He believed that its outcome depended on something besides the Father, or if He thought that the Father had to make a certain choice necessarily, that is, willy-nilly?

But at the same time, while we examine the words with which Christ begged His Father to avert His death and humbly submitted everything to the will of His Father, we must also constantly bear in mind that though He was both God and man, He said all these things not as God but insofar as He was man. We ourselves provide a parallel: because we are composed of body and soul, we sometimes apply to our whole selves things which actually are true only of the soul, and on the other hand we sometimes speak of our selves when strict accuracy would require us to speak of our bodies alone. For we say that the martyrs go straight to heaven when they die, whereas actually only their souls are taken up to heaven. And on the other hand we say that men, however proud they may be, are still only dust and ashes and that when they have finished with this brief life they will rot in a common ordinary grave. We constantly talk this way, even though the soul does not enter into the grave or undergo death but rather outlives the body, either in miserable torment if it lived badly while in the body, or else in perpetual well-being if it lived well.

In a similar fashion, then, Christ speaks of what He did as God and what He did as man, not as if He were divided into two persons but as one and the same person, and that rightly, since He was one person; for in the omnipotent person of Christ humanity and divinity were joined and made one no less closely than His immortal soul was united to a body which could die. Thus because of His divinity He did not hesitate to say, "I and the Father are one" and "Before Abraham came to be, I am." Moreover, because of both His natures, He said, "I am with you all days, even to the end of the world." And conversely, because of His humanity alone He said, "The Father is greater than I" and "A little while I am with you." It is true, of course, that His glorious body is really present with us, and always will be till the end of the world, under the appearance of bread in the venerable sacrament of the Eucharist; but that bodily form in which He once associated with His disciples (and this is the kind of presence He had in mind when He said, "A little while I am with you") was taken away after Christ's ascension, unless He Himself chooses to show it to someone, as He sometimes does.

Therefore, in this passage about Christ's agony, whichever of these deeds, sufferings, or prayers of His are so lowly that they seem quite incompatible with the lofty height of divinity, let us remember that the same Christ performed them as a man. Indeed, some of them had their origin only in the lower part of His humanity (I mean the part concerned with sensation), and these served to proclaim the genuineness of His human nature and to relieve the natural fears of other men in later times. Nothing, then, in these words, or in any of all the other things that the sequence of His agony presented as signs of His afflicted humanity, was considered by Christ to be unworthy of His glory; indeed, so little did He think so that He Himself took special care to see that they became widely known.

For though everything written by all the apostles was dictated throughout by one and the same spirit of Christ, still I find it hard to recall any of His other deeds which He took such particular pains to preserve in the memories of men. To be sure, He told His apostles about His intense sadness, so that they might be able to hand it down from Him to posterity. But the words of His prayer to His Father they could hardly have heard even if they had been awake (since the nearest of them were a stone's throw away), and even if they had been present when it happened, they still could not have heard because they were asleep. Certainly they would have been even less able, at that time of night, to make out when He knelt down or when He threw Himself face forward on the ground. As for those drops of blood which flowed like sweat from His whole body, even if they had later clearly seen the stain left on the ground, I think they would have drawn almost any number of conclusions without guessing the right one, since it was an unprecedented phenomenon for anyone to sweat blood.

Yet in the ensuing time before His death it seems unlikely that He spoke of these things either to His mother or to the apostles, unless one is willing to believe that He told the apostles the whole story of His agony when He left off praying and came back to them—that is, while they were either still sleeping or barely awake and quite drowsy—or else that He told them at the very time when the troops were at hand. The remaining alternative, then, and the one that seems most likely to be true, is that after He rose from the dead and there could no longer be any doubt that He was God, His most loving mother and beloved disciples heard from His own most holy lips this detailed account, point by point, of His human suffering, the knowledge of which would benefit both them and (through them) others who would come after them, and which no one could have recounted except Christ Himself. Therefore, to those whose hearts are troubled, meditation on this agony provides great consolation, and rightly so, since it was for this very purpose—to console the afflicted—that our Savior in His kindness made known His own affliction, which no one else knew or could have known.

Some may be concerned about another point: when Christ came back from that prayer to see His apostles and found them sleeping and so startled by His arrival that they did not know what to say, He left them, so that it might seem He had come only for the purpose of finding out whether they were awake, whereas He could not have lacked this knowledge (insofar as He was God) even before He came.

The answer to such persons, if there are any, should be this: nothing that He did was done in vain. It is true that His coming into their presence did not rouse them to complete vigilance but only to such a startled, half-waking drowsiness that they hardly raised their eyes to look at Him; or else (what is worse yet) if His reproaches did wake them up completely, still they slipped back into sleep the moment He went away. Nevertheless, He Himself both demonstrated His anxious concern for His disciples and also by His example gave to the future pastors of His church a solemn injunction not to allow themselves the slightest wavering, out of sadness or weariness or fear, in their diligent care of their flock, but rather to conduct themselves so as to prove in actual fact that they are not so much concerned for themselves as for the welfare of their flock.

But perhaps some meticulous fussy dissector of the divine plan might say: "Either Christ wished the apostles to stay awake or He did not. If He did not, why did He give such an explicit command? If He did, what use was there in going back and forth so often? Since He was God, could He not at one and the same time speak the command and ensure its execution?"

Doubtless He could have, my good man, since He was God, who carried out whatever He wished, who created all things with a word. He spoke and it was done, He commanded and they were created [Ps 33:9], He opened the

eyes of a man blind from birth; could He not, then, find a
way to open the eyes of a man who was asleep? Clearly,
even someone who was not God could easily do that. For
anyone can see that if you merely prick the eyes of sleepy
men with a tiny pin, they will stay awake and will certainly not go right back to sleep.

Doubtless Christ could have caused the apostles not to
sleep at all but to stay awake, if that had been what He
wished in an absolute and unqualified sense. But actually
His wish was modified by a condition—namely, that they
themselves wish to do so, and wish it so effectually that
each of them do his very best to comply with the outward
command Christ Himself gave and to cooperate with the
promptings of His inward assistance. In this way He also
wishes for all men to be saved and for no one to suffer eternal torment, that is, always provided that we conform to
His most loving will and do not set ourselves against it
through our own willful malice. If someone stubbornly
insists on doing this, God does not wish to waft him off to
heaven against his will, as if He were in need of our services there and could not continue His glorious reign without our support. Indeed, if He could not reign without us,
He would immediately punish many offenses which now,
out of consideration for us, He tolerates and overlooks for
a long time to see if His kindness and patience will bring
us to repent. But we meanwhile abuse this great mercy of
His by adding sins to sins, thus heaping up for ourselves
(as the apostle says) a treasure of wrath on the day of
wrath [Rom 2:5].

Nevertheless, such is God's kindness that even when
we are negligent and slumbering on the pillow of our sins,
He disturbs us from time to time, shakes us, strikes us, and
does His best to wake us up by means of tribulations. But
still, even though He thus proves Himself to be most loving even in His anger, most of us in our gross human stu-

pidity misinterpret His action and imagine that such a
great benefit is an injury, whereas actually (if we have any
sense) we should feel bound to pray frequently and fervently that whenever we wander away from Him He may
use blows to drive us back to the right way, even though
we are unwilling and struggle against Him.

Thus we must first pray that we may see the way and
with the Church we must say to God, "From blindness of
heart deliver us, O Lord." And with the prophet we must
say, "Teach me to do your will" and "Show me your ways
and teach me your paths." Then we must intensely desire
to run after you eagerly, O God, in the odor of your oint-
ments, in the most sweet scent of your Spirit. But if we
grow weary along the way (as we almost always do) and
lag so far behind that we barely manage to follow at a distance, let us immediately say to God, "Take my right
hand" and "Lead me along your path."

Then if we are so overcome by weariness that we no
longer have the heart to go on, if we are so soft and lazy
that we are about to stop altogether, let us beg God to drag
us along even as we struggle not to go. Finally, if we resist
when He draws us on gently and are stiff-necked against
the will of God, against our own salvation, utterly irra-
tional like horses and mules which have no intellects, we
ought to beseech God humbly in the most fitting words of
the prophet: "Hold my jaws hard, O God, with a bridle
and bit when I do not draw near to you" [Ps 32:9].

But then, since fondness for prayer is the first of our
virtues to go when we are overtaken by sloth, and since we
are reluctant to pray for anything (however useful) that we
are reluctant to receive, certainly if we have any sense at all
we ought to take this weakness into account well in
advance, before we fall into such sick and troubled states
of mind—we ought, in other words, to pour out to God
unceasingly such prayers as I have mentioned, and we

should humbly implore Him that if at some later time we should ask for anything untoward—allured, perhaps, by the enticements of the flesh, or seduced by a longing for worldly things, or overthrown by the clever snares of the devils—He may be deaf to such prayers and avert what we pray for, showering upon us instead those things He knows will be good for us, however much we beg Him to take them away. In fact, this is the way we normally act (if we are wise) when we are expecting a fever: we give advance warning to those who are to take care of us in our sickness that even if we beg them, they should not give us any of those things which our diseased condition makes us perversely long for though they are harmful to our health and only make the disease worse.

And when we are so fast asleep in our vices that even the calls and stirrings of divine mercy do not make us willing to rouse ourselves and wake up to virtuous living, we ourselves sometimes supply the reason why God goes away and leaves us to our vices; some He leaves so as never to come back again, but others He lets sleep only until another time, according as He sees fit in His wondrous kindness and the inscrutable depths of His wisdom.

Christ's action provided a sort of paradigm of this fact: when He went back to check on the apostles, they were unwilling to stay awake but rather went right on sleeping, and so He went away and left them. For "leaving them, He went away again and, kneeling down, said the same prayer in these words: 'Father, if you are willing, take this cup from me. Yet not my will but yours be done.' "

Notice how He again asks the same thing, again adds the same condition, again sets us an example to show that when we fall into great danger, even for God's sake, we should not think we are not allowed to beg God urgently to provide us a way out of that crisis. For one thing, it is quite possible that He permits us to be brought into such difficulties precisely because fear of danger makes us grow fervent in prayer when prosperity has made us cold, especially when it is a question of bodily danger—for most of us are not very warmly concerned about danger to our souls. Now as for those who are concerned (as they ought to be) about their souls, unless someone is strengthened and inspired by God to undergo martyrdom—a condition which must be either directly experienced in an unexplainable way or else judged by appropriate indications—apart from such a case everyone has sufficient grounds to be afraid that he may grow weary under his burden and give in. Hence everyone, to avoid such overconfidence as Peter's, ought to pray diligently that God in His goodness may deliver him from such a great danger to his soul. But it must be stressed again and again that no one should pray to escape danger so absolutely that he would not be willing to leave the whole matter up to God, ready in all obedience to endure what God has prepared for him.

These are some of the reasons, then, why Christ provided us with this salutary example of prayer. Not that He Himself was in any need of such prayer—nothing could be further from the truth. For insofar as He was God, He was not inferior to the Father. Insofar as He was God, not only His power but also His will was the same as the Father's. Certainly insofar as He was man, His power was infinitely less, but then all power, both in heaven and on earth, was finally given to Him by the Father [Mt 28:18]. And though His will, insofar as He was man, was not identical with the Father's, still it was in such complete conformity with the will of the Father that no disagreement was ever found between them.

Thus the reasoning power of His soul, in obedience to the will of the Father, agrees to suffer that most bitter death while at the same time, as a proof of His humanity, His bodily senses react to the prospect with revulsion and dread. His prayer expresses vividly both the fear and the obedience: "Father," He said, "if you are willing, take this cup from me. Yet not my will but yours be done."

His deeds, however, present this dual reaction even more clearly than His words. That His reasoning faculties never drew back from such horrible torture but rather remained obedient to the Father even to death, even to the death of the cross, was demonstrated by the succeeding events of the passion. And that His feelings were overwhelmed by an intense fear of His coming passion is shown by the words which come next in the Gospel.

And there appeared to Him an angel from heaven to strengthen Him. [Lk 22:43]
Do you realize how intense His mental anguish must have been, that an angel should come from heaven to strengthen Him?

But when I consider this passage, I cannot help wondering what pernicious nonsense has gotten into the heads of those who contend that it is futile for anyone to seek the intercession of any angel or departed saint, namely, on the grounds that we can confidently address our prayers to God Himself, not only because He alone is more present to us than all the angels and all the saints put together but also because He has the power to grant us more, and a greater desire to do so, than any of the saints in heaven, of whatever description.

With such trivial and groundless arguments as these, they express their envious displeasure at the glory of the saints, who are in turn equally displeased with such men; for they strive to undermine the loving homage we pay to the saints and the saving assistance they render to us. Why should these shameless men not follow the same line of reasoning here and argue that the angel's effort to offer consolation to our Savior Christ was utterly pointless and superfluous? For what angel of them all was as powerful as He Himself or as near to Him as God, since He Himself was God? But in fact, just as He wished to undergo sadness and anxiety for our sake, so too for our sake He wished to have an angel console Him, for a number of reasons: both to refute the foolish arguments of such men and to make it clear that He was truly man (for just as angels ministered to Him as God when He had triumphed over the temptations of the devil, so too an angel came to console Him as man while He was making His lowly progress toward death) and, moreover, to give us hope that if we direct our prayers to God when we are in danger, we cannot lack consolation—always provided we do not pray in a lazy and perfunctory way, but rather imitate Christ in this passage by sighing and praying from the bottom of our hearts.

"For in His agony He prayed more earnestly, and His sweat became like drops of blood running down to the ground." [Lk 22:44]

Most scholars affirm that what Christ suffered for us was more painful than the suffering of any of all the martyrs, of whatever time or place, who underwent martyrdom for the faith. But others disagree, because there are various other sorts of torture than those to which Christ was subjected and some torments have been extended over a period of several days, a longer time than those of Christ lasted. Then too, they think that since one drop of Christ's precious blood, because of His infinite divinity, would have been far more than enough to redeem all mankind, therefore His ordeal was not ordained by God according to the standards of anyone else's suffering but according to the proper measure of His own unfathomable wisdom. And since no one can know this measure with certainty, they hold that it is not prejudicial to the faith to believe that Christ's pain was less than that of some of the martyrs. But as for me, apart from the widespread opinion of the Church which fittingly applies to Christ Jeremiah's words about Jerusalem ("O all you who pass by the way, look and see if there is any sorrow like mine" [Lam 1:12]), certainly I find that this passage also provides very convincing reasons to believe that no martyr's torments could ever be compared with Christ's suffering, even on this point of the intensity of the pain.

Even if I should grant what I have good reasons to think need not be granted, namely, that any of the martyrs was subjected to more kinds of torture and greater ones, even (if you like) longer ones than Christ endured, still I find it not at all hard to believe that tortures which to all appearances may be considerably less fierce actually caused Christ to suffer more excruciating pain than someone might feel from tortures that seem much more grievous, and for this reason: I see that Christ, as the thought of His coming passion was borne in upon Him, was overwhelmed by mental anguish more bitter than any other mortal has ever experienced from the thought of coming torments. For who has ever felt such bitter anguish that a bloody sweat broke out all over his body and ran down in drops to the ground? The intensity of the actual pain itself, therefore, I estimate by this standard: I see that even the presentiment of it before it arrived was more bitter to Christ than such anticipation has ever been to anyone else.

Nor could this anguish of the mind ever have grown to sufficient intensity to cause the body to sweat blood if He had not, of His own free will, exercised His divine omnipotence not only to refrain from alleviating this painful pressure but even to add to its force and strength. This He did in order to prefigure the blood which future martyrs would be forced to pour forth on the ground, and at the same time to offer this unheard-of, this marvelous example of profound anguish as a consolation to those who would be so fearful and alarmed at the thought of torture that they might otherwise interpret their fear as a sign of their downfall and thus yield to despair.

At this point, if someone should again bring up those martyrs who freely and eagerly exposed themselves to death because of their faith in Christ, and if he should offer his opinion that they are especially worthy of the laurels of triumph because with a joy that left no room for sorrow they betrayed no trace of sadness, no sign of fear, I am perfectly willing to go along with him on that point, so long as he does not go so far as to deny the triumph of those who do not rush forth of their own accord but who nevertheless do not hang back or withdraw once they have been seized, but rather go on in spite of their fearful anxiety and face the terrible prospect out of love for Christ.

Now if anyone should argue that the eager martyrs receive a greater share of glory than the others, I have no objection—he can have the argument all to himself. For I rest content with the fact that in heaven neither sort of martyr will lack a glory so great that while they were alive their eyes never saw the like, nor did their ears ever hear it, nor did it ever enter into their hearts [to conceive of it]. And even if someone does have a higher place in heaven, no one else envies him for it—quite the opposite, everyone enjoys the glory of everyone else because of their mutual love.

Besides, just who outranks whom in the glory assigned by God in heaven is not, I think, quite crystal-clear to us, groping as we are in the darkness of our mortality.

For though I grant that God loves a cheerful giver, still I have no doubt that He loved Tobias and holy Job too. Now it is true that both of them bore their calamities bravely and patiently, but neither of them, so far as I know, was exactly jumping with joy or clapping his hands out of happiness.

To expose one's self to death for Christ's sake when the case clearly demands it or when God gives a secret prompting to do so, this, I do not deny, is a deed of preeminent virtue. But otherwise I do not think it very safe to do so, and among those who willingly suffered for Christ we find outstanding figures who were very much afraid, who were deeply distressed, who even withdrew from death more than once before they finally faced it bravely.

Certainly I do not mean to derogate from God's power to inspire martyrs; indeed I believe that He exercises it on occasion (either granting this favor to holy persons as a reward for the labors of their past lives or giving it purely and simply out of His own generosity) by filling the whole mind of a martyr with such joy that he not only wards off those grievous emotional disturbances but also keeps himself completely free from what the Stoics call "incipient emotions," freely admitting that even their factitious wise men are susceptible to them.

Since we often see it happen that some men do not feel wounds inflicted in battle until their awareness, which had been displaced by strong feeling, returns to them and they notice the injury, certainly there is no reason why I should doubt that a mind exulting in the high hopes of approaching glory can be so rapt and transported beyond itself that it neither fears death nor feels torments.

But still, even if God did give someone this gift, I would certainly be inclined to call it an unearned felicity or the recompense of past virtue, but not the measure of future reward in heaven. Now I might have believed that this future reward corresponds to the pain suffered for Christ, except that God in His generosity bestows it in such good measure—so full, so concentrated, so overflowing—that the sufferings of this time are by no means worthy to be compared to that future glory which will be revealed in those who loved God so dearly that they spent their very life's blood for His glory, with such mental agony and bodily torment. Besides, is it not possible that God in His goodness removes fear from some persons not because He approves of or intends to reward their boldness, but rather because He is aware of their weakness and knows that they would not be equal to facing fear? For some have yielded to fear, even though they won out later when the actual tortures were inflicted.

Now as for the point that those who eagerly suffer death encourage others by their example, I would not deny that for many they provide a very useful pattern. But on the other hand, since almost all of us are fearful in the face of death, who can know how many have also been helped by those whom we see face death with fear and trembling but whom we also observe as they break bravely through the hindrances blocking their path, the obstacles barring their way with barriers harder than steel—that is, their own weariness, fear, and anguish—and by bursting these iron bars and triumphing over death take heaven by storm? Seeing them, will not weaklings who are, like them, cowardly and afraid take heart so as not to yield under the stress of persecution even though they feel great sadness welling up within them, and fear and weariness and horror at the prospect of a ghastly death?

Thus the wisdom of God, which penetrates all things irresistibly and disposes all things sweetly, foreseeing and contemplating in His ever-present sight how the minds of men in different places would be affected, suits His examples to various times and places, choosing now one destiny, now another, according as He sees which will be most profitable. And so God proportions the temperaments of His martyrs according to His own providence in such a way that one rushes forth eagerly to his death, another

creeps out hesitantly and fearfully but for all that bears his
death none the less bravely—unless someone perhaps
imagines he ought to be thought less brave for having
fought down not only his other enemies but also his own
weariness, sadness, and fear—most strong feelings and
mighty enemies indeed.

But the whole drift of the present discussion finally
comes to this: we should admire both kinds of most holy
martyrs; we should venerate both kinds, praise God for
both; we should imitate both when the situation demands
it, each according to his own capacity and according to the
grace God gives to each.

But the person who is conscious of his own eagerness
needs not so much encouragement to be daring as perhaps
a reminder to be afraid lest his presumption, like Peter's,
lead to a sudden relapse and fall. But if a person feels anxious, heavy-hearted, fearful, certainly he ought to be com-
forted and encouraged to take heart. For both sorts of martyrs this anguish of Christ is most salutary: it keeps the one
from being over-exultant, and it makes the other be of
good hope when his spirit is crestfallen and downcast. For
if anyone feels his mind swelling with ungovernable
enthusiasm, perhaps when he recalls this lowly and
anguished bearing of his commander he will have reason
to fear, lest our sly enemy is lifting him up on high for a
while so that a little later he can dash him to the ground all
the harder. But whoever is utterly crushed by feelings of
anxiety and fear and is tortured by the fear that he may
yield to despair, let him consider this agony of Christ, let
him meditate on it constantly and turn it over in his mind,
let him drink deep and health-giving draughts of consolation from this spring. For here he will see the loving Shepherd lifting the weak lamb on His shoulders playing the
same role as he himself does, expressing his very own feelings, and for this reason: so that anyone who later feels

himself disturbed by similar feelings might take courage and not think that he must despair.

Therefore let us give Him as many thanks as we can (for certainly we can never give Him enough); and in our agony remembering His (with which no other can ever be compared), let us beg Him with all our strength that He may deign to comfort us in our anguish by an insight into His; and when we urgently beseech Him, because of our mental distress, to free us from danger, let us nevertheless follow His own most wholesome example by concluding our prayer with His own addition: "Yet not as I will but as you will." If we do these things diligently, I have no doubt at all that just as an angel brought Him consolation in answer to His prayer, so too each of our angels will bring us from His Spirit consolation that will give us the strength to persevere in those deeds that will lift us up to heaven. And in order to make us completely confident of this fact, Christ went there before us by the same method, by the same path. For after He had suffered this agony for a long time, His spirits were so restored that He arose, returned to His apostles, and freely went out to meet the traitor and the tormentors who were seeking Him to make Him suffer. Then, when He had suffered (as was necessary), He entered into His glory, preparing there a place also for those of us who follow in His footsteps. And lest we should be deprived of it by our own dullness, may He Himself because of His own agony deign to help us in ours.

And when He had arisen from prayer and come to His disciples, He found them sleeping for sadness, and He said to them, "Why are you sleeping? Sleep on now and take your rest. That is enough. Get up and pray that you may not enter into temptation. Behold, the hour is coming when the Son of Man will be betrayed into the hands of sinners. Get up, let us go. Behold, the one who will betray me is near at hand." *[Mt 26:45-46, Mk 14:41-42]*

See now, when Christ comes back to His apostles for the third time, there they are, buried in sleep, though He commanded them to bear up with Him and to stay awake and pray because of the impending danger; but Judas the traitor at the same time was so wide awake and intent on betraying the Lord that the very idea of sleep never entered his mind.

Does not this contrast between the traitor and the apostles present to us a clear and sharp mirror image (as it were), a sad and terrible view of what has happened through the ages from those times even to our own? Why do not bishops contemplate in this scene their own somnolence? Since they have succeeded in the place of the apostles, would that they would reproduce their virtues just as eagerly as they embrace their authority and as faithfully as they display their sloth and sleepiness! For very many are sleepy and apathetic in sowing virtues among the people and maintaining the truth, while the enemies of Christ, in order to sow vices and uproot the faith (that is, insofar as they can, to seize Christ and cruelly crucify Him once again), are wide awake—so much wiser (as Christ says) are the sons of darkness in their generation than the sons of light.

But although this comparison of the sleeping apostles applies very well to those bishops who sleep while virtue and the faith are placed in jeopardy, still it does not apply to all such prelates at all points. For some of them—alas, far more than I could wish—do not drift into sleep through sadness and grief as the apostles did. Rather, they are numbed and buried in destructive desires; that is, drunk with the new wine of the devil, the flesh, and the world, they sleep like pigs sprawling in the mire. Certainly the apostles' feeling of sadness because of the danger to their Master was praiseworthy, but for them to be so overcome

by sadness as to yield completely to sleep, that was certainly wrong. Even to grieve because the world is perishing or
to weep because of the crimes of others bespeaks a reverent outlook, as was felt by the writer who said, "I sat by
myself and groaned" [Lam 3:28] and also by the one who
said, "I was sick at heart because of sinners abandoning
your law" [Ps 119:53]. Sadness of this sort I would place in
the category of which he says, ["For the sorrow that is
according to God produces repentance that surely tends to
salvation, whereas the sorrow that is according to the
world produces death" (2 Cor 7:10)]. But I would place it
there only if the feeling, however good, is checked by the
rule and guidance of reason. For if this is not the case, if
sorrow so grips the mind that its strength is sapped and
reason gives up the reins, if a bishop is so overcome by
heavy-hearted sleep that he neglects to do what the duty of
his office requires for the salvation of his flock—like a cowardly ship's captain who is so disheartened by the furious
din of a storm that he deserts the helm, hides away cowering in some cranny, and abandons the ship to the waves—
if a bishop does this, I would certainly not hesitate to juxtapose and compare his sadness with the sadness that leads,
as [Paul] says, to hell; indeed, I would consider it far
worse, since such sadness in religious matters seems to
spring from a mind which despairs of God's help.

The next category, but a far worse one, consists of
those who are not depressed by sadness at the danger of
others but rather by a fear of injury to themselves, a fear
which is so much the worse as its cause is the more contemptible, that is, when it is not a question of life or death
but of money.

And yet Christ commands us to contemn the loss of
the body itself for His sake. "Do not be afraid," He says,
"of those who destroy the body and after that can do nothing further. But I will show you the one you should fear,

the one to fear: fear Him who, when He has destroyed the body, has the power to send the soul also to hell. This, I tell you, is the one you must fear."

And though He lays down this rule for everyone without exception when they have been seized and there is no way out, He attaches a separate charge over and above this to the high office of prelates: He does not allow them to be concerned only about their own souls or merely to take refuge in silence until they are dragged out and forced to choose between open profession or lying dissimulation, but He also wished them to come forth if they see that the flock entrusted to them is in danger and to face the danger of their own accord for the good of their flock. "The good shepherd," says Christ, "lays down his life for his sheep." But if every good shepherd lays down his life for his sheep, certainly one who saves his own life to the detriment of his sheep is not fulfilling the role of a good shepherd.

Therefore, just as one who loses his life for Christ (and he does this if he loses it for the flock of Christ entrusted to him) saves it for life everlasting, so too one who denies Christ (and this he does if he fails to profess the truth when his silence injures his flock) by saving his life, he actually proceeds to lose it. Clearly it is even worse if, driven by fear, he denies Christ openly in words and forsakes Him publicly. Such prelates do not sleep like Peter, they make his waking denial. But under the kindly glance of Christ, most of them through His grace will eventually wipe out that failure and save themselves by weeping, if only they respond to His glance and friendly call to repentance with bitterness of heart and a new way of life, remembering His words and contemplating His passion and leaving behind the shackles of evil which bound them in their sins.

But if anyone is so set in evil that he does not merely neglect to profess the truth out of fear but like Arius and his ilk preaches false doctrine, whether for sordid gain or out of a corrupt ambition, such a person does not sleep like Peter, does not make Peter's denial, but rather stays awake with wicked Judas and like Judas persecutes Christ. This man's condition is far more dangerous than that of the others, as is shown by the sad and horrible end Judas came to. But since there is no limit to the kindness of a merciful God, even this sort of sinner ought not to despair of forgiveness. Even to Judas God gave many opportunities of coming to his senses. He did not deny him His companionship. He did not take away from him the dignity of his apostleship. He did not even take the purse-strings from him, even though he was a thief. He admitted the traitor to the fellowship of His beloved disciples at the Last Supper. He deigned to stoop down at the feet of the betrayer and to wash with His innocent and most sacred hands Judas' dirty feet, a most fit symbol of his filthy mind. Moreover, with incomparable generosity He gave him to eat, in the form of bread, that very body of His which the betrayer had already sold; and under the appearance of wine, He gave him that very blood to drink which, even while he was drinking it, the traitor was wickedly scheming to broach and set flowing. Finally, when Judas, coming with his crew to seize Him, offered Him a kiss, a kiss that was in fact the terrible token of his treachery, Christ received him calmly and gently. Who would not believe that any one of all these could have turned the traitor's mind, however hardened in crime, to better courses? Then too, even that beginning of repentance, when he admitted he had sinned and gave back the pieces of silver and threw them away when they were not accepted, crying out that he was a traitor and confessing that he had betrayed innocent blood—I am inclined to believe that Christ prompted him thus far so that He might if possible (that is, if the traitor did not add despair to his treachery) save from ruin the very man who had so recently, so perfidiously, betrayed Him to death.

Therefore, since God showed His great mercy in so many ways even toward Judas, an apostle turned traitor, since He invited him to forgiveness so often and did not allow him to perish except through despair alone, certainly there is no reason why, in this life, anyone should despair of any imitator of Judas. Rather, according to that holy advice of the apostle "Pray for each other that you may be saved" [Jms 5:16], if we see anyone wandering wildly from the right road, let us hope that he will one day return to the path, and meanwhile let us pray humbly and incessantly that God will hold out to him chances to come to his senses, and likewise that with God's help he will eagerly seize them, and having seized them will hold fast and not throw them away out of malice or let them slip away from him through wretched sloth.

And so when Christ had found His apostles sleeping for the third time, He said to them, "Why are you sleeping?"—as if to say: "Now is not the time to sleep. Now is the crucial time for you to stay awake and pray, as I myself have already warned you twice before, only a little while ago." And as for them, since they did not know what to reply to Him when He found them sleeping for the second time, what suitable excuse could they possibly have devised now that they had been so quickly caught in the same fault for the third time? Could they use as an excuse what the evangelist mentions—that is, could they say they were sleeping because of their sadness? Certainly the fact is mentioned by Luke, but it is also quite clear that he does not praise it. It is true, he does suggest that their sadness itself was praiseworthy, as it certainly was. Still, the sleep that followed from it was not free of moral blame. For the sort of sadness that is potentially worthy of great reward sometimes tends toward great evil. Certainly it does if we are so taken up by it that we render it useless—that is, if

we do not have recourse to God with our petitions and
prayers and seek comfort from Him, but instead, in a certain downcast and desperate frame of mind, try to escape
our awareness of sadness by looking for consolation in
sleep. Nor will we find what we are looking for: losing in
sleep the consolation we might have obtained from God by
staying awake and praying, we feel the weary weight of a
troubled mind even during sleep itself, and also we stum-
ble with our eyes closed into temptations and the traps set
by the devil.

And so Christ, as if He intended to preclude any
excuse for this sleepiness, said, "'Why are you sleeping?
Sleep on now and take your rest. That is enough. Get up
and pray that you may not enter into temptation. Behold,
the hour has almost come when the Son of Man will be
betrayed into the hands of sinners. Get up, let us go.
Behold, the one who will betray me is near at hand.' And
while Jesus was still speaking, behold Judas Iscariot...."

Immediately after He had aroused the sleeping apostles for the third time, He undercut them with irony: not
indeed that trivial and sportive variety with which idle
men of wit are accustomed to amuse themselves, but rather
a serious and weighty kind of irony. "'Sleep on now,' He
said, 'and take your rest. That is enough. Get up and pray
that you may not enter into temptation. Behold, the hour
has almost come when the Son of Man will be betrayed
into the hands of sinners. Get up, let us go. Behold, the one
who will betray me is near at hand.' And while He was
still speaking, Judas...."

Notice how He grants permission to sleep in such a
way as clearly shows He means to take it away. For He had
hardly said, "Sleep" before He added, "That is enough"—
as if to say: "Now there is no need for you to sleep any
longer. It is enough that throughout the whole time you
ought to have been staying awake, you have been sleep-

ing—and that even against my direct orders. Now there is no time left to sleep, not even to sit down. You must get up immediately and pray that you may not enter into temptation, the temptation, perhaps, of deserting me and giving great scandal by doing so. Otherwise, so far as sleep is concerned, sleep on now and take your rest—you have my permission—that is, if you can. But you will certainly not be able to. For there are people coming—they are almost here—who will shake the yawning sleepiness out of you. For behold, the hour has almost come when the Son of Man will be betrayed into the hands of sinners, and behold, the one who will betray me is near at hand." "And He had hardly finished these few admonitions and was still speaking when, behold, Judas Iscariot...."

I am not unaware that some learned and holy men do not allow this interpretation, though they admit that others, equally learned and holy, have found it agreeable. Not that those who do not accept this interpretation are shocked by this sort of irony, as some others are—also pious men, to be sure, but not sufficiently versed in the figures of speech which sacred Scripture customarily takes over from common speech. For if they were, they would have found irony in so many other places that they could not have found it offensive here.

What could be more pungent or witty than the irony with which the blessed apostle gracefully polishes off the Corinthians?—I mean where he asks pardon because he never burdened any of them with charges and expenses: "For how have I done any less for you than for the other churches, except this, that I have never been a burden to you? Pardon me for this injustice" [2 Cor 12:13]. What could be more forceful or biting than the irony with which God's prophet ridiculed the prophets of Baal as they called upon the deaf statue of their god?— "Call louder," he said, "for your god is asleep or perhaps has gone somewhere on

a trip" [1 Kgs 18:27]. I have taken this occasion to bring up
these instances in passing because some readers, out of a
certain pious simplicity, refuse to accept in sacred Scripture (or at least do not notice there) these universally used
forms of speech, and by neglecting the figures of speech
they very often also miss the real sense of Scripture.

Now concerning this passage, St. Augustine says that
he finds the interpretation I have given to be not unaccept-
able but also not necessary. He claims that the plain meaning without any figure is adequate. He presents such an
interpretation of this passage in the work he wrote entitled
The Harmony of the Gospels. "It seems," he says, "that the
language of Matthew here is self-contradictory. For how
could He say, 'Sleep on now and take your rest' and then
immediately add, 'Get up, let us go'? Disturbed by this
seeming inconsistency, some try to set the tone of the words
'Sleep on now and take your rest' as reproachful rather
than permissive. And this would be the right thing to do if
it were necessary. But Mark reports it in such a way that
when Christ had said, 'Sleep on now and take your rest,'
He added, 'That is enough' and then went on to say, 'The
hour has come when the Son of Man will be betrayed.'
Therefore it is surely at least implied that after He had said,
'Sleep and take your rest,' the Lord was silent for a while so
that they could do what He had allowed them to do, and
that He then went on to say, 'Behold, the hour has almost
come.' That is the reason why Mark includes 'That is
enough,' that is, 'You have rested long enough.' "

Subtle indeed this reasoning of the most blessed
Augustine, as he always is; but I imagine that those of the
opposite persuasion do not find it at all likely that after
Christ had already reproached them twice for sleeping
when His capture was imminent, and after He had just
rebuked them sternly by saying, "Why are you sleeping?"
He should then have granted them time to sleep, especially

at the very time when the danger which was the reason they ought not to have slept before was now pounding on the door, as they say. But now that I have presented both interpretations, everyone is free to choose whichever he likes. My purpose has been merely to recount both of them; it is not for such a nobody as me to render a decision like an official arbitrator.

"Get up and pray that you may not enter into temptation."
[Lk 22:46]

Before, He ordered them to watch and pray. Now that they have twice learned by experience that the drowsy position of sitting lets sleep gradually slip up on them, He teaches an instant remedy for that sluggish disease of somnolence, namely, to get up. Since this sort of remedy was handed down by our Savior Himself, I heartily wish that we would occasionally be willing to try it out at the dead of night. For here we would discover not only that well begun is half done (as Horace says), but that once begun is all done.

For when we are fighting against sleep, the first encounter is always the sharpest. Therefore we should not try to conquer sleep by a prolonged struggle, but rather we should break with one thrust the grip of the alluring arms with which it embraces us and pulls us down, and we should dash away from it all of a sudden. Then once we have cast off idle sleep, the very image of death, life with its eagerness will resume its sway. Then if we devote ourselves to meditation and prayer, the mind, collected and composed in that dark silence of the night, will find that it is much more receptive to divine consolation than it is during the daytime, when the noisy bustle of business on all sides distracts the eyes, the ears, and the mind and dissipates our energy in manifold activities, no less pointless than they are diverse. But Lord spare us, though thoughts about some trifling matter, some worldly matter at that, may sometimes interrupt our sleep and keep us awake for a long time and hardly let us go back to sleep at all, prayer does not keep us awake: in spite of the immense loss of spiritual benefits, in spite of the many traps set for us by our deadly enemy, in spite of the danger of being utterly undone, we do not wake up to pray, but lie in a drugged sleep watching the dream-visions induced by mandragora.

But we must continually keep in mind that Christ did not command them simply to get up, but to get up in order to pray. For it is not enough to get up if we do not get up for a good purpose. If we do not, there would be far less sin in losing time through slothful drowsiness than in devoting waking time to the deliberate pursuit of malicious crimes.

Then too, He does not merely order them to pray but shows them the need for it and teaches what they should have prayed for. "Pray," He says, "that you may not enter into temptation." Again and again He drove home this point to them, that prayer is the only safeguard against temptation and that if someone refuses it entrance into the castle of his soul and shuts it out by yielding to sleep, through such negligence he permits the besieging troops of the devil (that is, temptations to evil) to break in.

Three times He admonished them verbally to pray. Then, to avoid the appearance of teaching merely by these words and in order to teach them by His example as well, He Himself prayed three times, suggesting in this way that we ought to pray to the Trinity, namely, to the unbegotten Father, to the coequal Son begotten by Him, and to the Spirit equal to each and proceeding from each of them. From these three we should likewise pray for three things: forgiveness for the past, grace to manage the present, and a prudent concern for the future. But we should pray for these things not lazily and carelessly but incessantly and fervently. Just how far from this kind of prayer nearly all of us are nowadays, everyone can judge privately from his own conscience and we may all publicly learn (God forbid) by the decreasing fruits of prayer, falling off gradually from day to day.

Nevertheless, since a little earlier I bore down on this point as vigorously as I could by attacking that sort of prayer in which the mind is not attentive but wandering and distracted among many ideas, it would be well at this point to propose an emollient from Gerson to alleviate this sore point, lest I seem to be like a harsh surgeon touching this common sore too roughly, bringing to many tender-souled mortals not a healing medicine but rather pain, and taking away from them hope of attaining salvation. In order to cure these troublesome inflammations of the soul, Gerson uses certain palliatives which are analogous to those medications which doctors use to relieve bodily pain and which they call "anodynes."

And so this John Gerson, an outstanding scholar and a most gentle handler of troubled consciences, saw (I imagine) some people whom this distraction of mind made so terribly anxious that they repeated the individual words of their prayers one after the other with a belabored sort of babbling and still got nowhere, and sometimes were even less pleased with their prayer the third time than the first time. He saw that such people, through sheer weariness, lost all sense of consolation from their prayers and that some of them were ready to give up the habit of prayer as useless (if they were to pray in this way) or even harmful (as they feared). This kind man, then, in order to relieve them of their troublesome difficulty, pointed out three aspects of prayer: the act, the virtue, and the habit.

But to make his meaning clearer, he explains it by the example of a person setting out from France on a pilgrimage to St. James [of Compostella]. For such a person sometimes goes forward on his journey and at the same time meditates on the holy saint and the purpose of the pilgrimage. And so this man throughout this whole time continues his pilgrimage by a double act, namely (and I shall use Gerson's own words), by a "natural continuity" and a "moral continuity": natural, because he actually and in fact proceeds toward that place; moral, because his thoughts are occupied with the matter of his pilgrimage. By "moral" he refers to that moral intention by which the act of setting out, otherwise indifferent, is perfected by the pious reason for setting out.

Sometimes, however, the pilgrim goes his way considering other matters, without thinking anything about the saint or the place, thinking perhaps about something even holier, such as God Himself. In such a case he continues the act of his pilgrimage on a natural, but not a moral level. For though he actually moves his feet along, he does not actually think about the reason for setting out nor perhaps even about the way he is going. But though the moral act of his pilgrimage does not continue, its moral virtue does. For that whole natural act of walking is informed and imbued with a moral virtue because it is silently accompanied by the pious intention formed at the beginning, since all this motion follows from that first decision, just as a stone continues in its course because of the original impetus, even though the hand which threw it has been withdrawn.

Sometimes, however, the moral act takes place when there is no natural act, as, for example, whenever the person thinks about his pilgrimage when he is perhaps sitting and not walking. Finally, it often happens that both kinds of act are missing, as, for example, when we are sleeping, for then the pilgrim neither performs the natural act of walking nor the moral act of thinking about the pilgrimage; but still in the meantime the moral virtue, so long as it is not deliberately renounced, remains and persists habitually.

And so this pilgrimage is never truly interrupted in such a way that its merit does not continue and persist at least habitually unless an opposite decision is made, either to give up the pilgrimage completely or at least to put it off until another time. And so by means of this comparison he draws the same conclusions about prayer, namely, that once it has been begun attentively it can never afterwards be so interrupted that the virtue of the first intention does not remain and persist continuously—that is, either actually or habitually—so long as it is not relinquished by making a decision to stop nor cut off by turning away to mortal sin.

Hence he says that those words of Christ "You should pray always and not cease" [Lk 18:1] were not spoken figuratively but in a simple and straightforward sense, and that in fact they are actually and literally fulfilled by good men. He supports his opinion with that well-known adage of learned men "Whoever lives well is always praying"— which is true, because whoever does everything, according to the apostle's precept, for the glory of God [1 Cor 10:31], once he has begun praying attentively never afterwards interrupts his prayer in such a way that its meritorious virtue does not persist, if not actually then at least habitually.

This is the explanation given by that most learned and virtuous man John Gerson in his short treatise entitled *Prayer and its Value.* But nevertheless he intends it as a consolation for those who are troubled and saddened because their attention slips away from them unawares during prayer even though they are earnestly trying to pay attention; he does not intend that it should provide a flattering illusion of safety for those who out of careless laziness make no effort to think about their prayers. For when we perform such a grave duty negligently, we say prayers indeed but we do not pray, and we do not (as I said before) render God favorable to us but drive Him far from us in His wrath. And why should anyone be surprised if God is angry when He sees Himself addressed so contemptuously by a lowly human creature? And how can we imagine that a person does not approach and address God contemptuously when he says to God, "O God, hear my prayer," while his own mind all the time is turned away to other matters—vain and foolish and, would that they were not, sometimes also wicked matters—so that he does not even hear his own voice but murmurs his way by rote through well-worn prayers, his mind a complete blank, emitting (as Virgil says) sounds without sense. Thus when we have finished our prayers and gone our way, very often we are immediately in need of other prayers to beg forgiveness for our former carelessness.

And so when Christ had said to His apostles, "Get up and pray that you may not enter into temptation," He immediately warned them how great the impending danger was, in order to show that no drowsy or lukewarm prayer would suffice. "Behold," He said, "the hour has almost come when the Son of Man will be betrayed into the hands of sinners," as if to include the following implications: "I predicted to you that I must be betrayed by one of you—you were shocked at the very words. I foretold to you that Satan would seek you out to sift you like wheat— you heard this carelessly and made no response, as if his temptation were not much to be reckoned with. So that you might know that temptation is not at all to be contemned, I predicted that you would all be scandalized because of me—you all denied it. To him who denied it most of all, I predicted that he would deny me three times before the cock crowed—he absolutely insisted it would

not be so and that he would rather die with me than deny
me, and so you all said. Lest you should consider temptation a thing to be taken lightly, I again and again commanded you to watch and pray lest you enter into temptation—but you were always so far from recognizing the
strength of temptation that you took no pains to pray
against it or even to stay awake.

"Perhaps you were encouraged to scorn the power of
the devil's temptation by the fact that before, when I sent
you out two by two to preach the faith, you came back and
reported to me that even the demons were subject to you.
But I, to whom the nature of demons, as well as your own
nature, is more deeply known than either is to you, since
indeed I established each of them, I immediately cautioned
you not to glory in such vanity, because it was not your
power that subjected the demons but rather I myself did it;
and I did it not for your sakes but for the sake of others
who were to be converted to the faith; and I admonished
you rather to glory in a real source of joy, namely, that
your names are written in the book of life. This really and
truly belongs to you, because once you have attained that
joy you can never lose it, though all the ranks of the
demons should struggle against you. But still the power
you exerted against them at that time gave you such high
confidence that you seem to scorn their temptations as
matters of little moment.

"And so, though I foretold that there was danger
impending on this very night, up to now you have still
viewed these temptations, as it were, from a distance. But
now I warn you that not only the very night but even the
very hour is at hand. For behold, the hour has almost come
when the Son of Man will be betrayed into the hands of
sinners. Now, therefore, there is no more chance to sit and
sleep. Now you will be forced to stay awake, and there is
hardly a moment left to pray. Now, therefore, I no longer

foretell future events but I say to you right now, at this present moment: Get up, let us go—behold, the one who will betray me is at hand. If you are not willing to stay awake so that you might be able to pray, at least get up and go away quickly lest you be unable to escape. For behold, the one who will betray me is at hand"—unless perhaps He did not say, "Get up, let us go" as intending that they should run away in fear, but rather that they should go forward with confidence. For He Himself did so: He did not turn back in another direction, but even as He spoke He freely went on to encounter those butchers who were making their way toward Him with murder in their hearts. "While Jesus was still saying these things, behold, Judas Iscariot, one of the twelve, and with him a large crowd with swords and clubs, sent by the chief priests and the scribes and the elders of the people."

Although nothing can contribute more effectively to salvation and to the implanting of every sort of virtue in the Christian breast than pious and fervent meditation on the successive events of Christ's passion, still it would certainly be not unprofitable to take the story of that time when the apostles were sleeping as the Son of Man was being betrayed, and to apply it as a mysterious image of future times. For Christ, to redeem man, truly became a son of man—that is, although He was conceived without male seed, He was nevertheless really descended from the first men and therefore truly became a son of Adam, so that by His passion He might restore Adam's posterity, lost and cast off into wretchedness through the fault of our first parents, to a state of happiness even greater than their original one. This is the reason that in spite of His divinity He constantly called Himself the Son of Man (since He was also really a man), thus constantly suggesting, by mentioning that nature which alone was capable of death, the benefit we derive from His death. For though God died, since

He who was God died, nevertheless His divinity did not undergo death but only His humanity, or actually only His body, if we consider the fact of nature more than the custom of language. For a man is said to die when the soul leaves the dead body, but the soul which departs is itself immortal. But since He did not merely delight in the phrase describing our nature but was also pleased to take upon Himself our nature for our salvation, and then finally to unite with Himself, in the structure of one body (as it were), all of us whom He regenerated by His saving sacraments and by faith, granting us a share even of His names (since Scripture calls all the faithful both gods [Jn 10:34-35] and Christs [Ps 105:15]), I think we would not be far wrong if we were to fear that the time approaches when the Son of Man, Christ, will be betrayed into the hands of sinners as often as we see an imminent danger that the mystical body of Christ, the church of Christ, namely, the Christian people, will be brought to ruin at the hands of wicked men. And this, alas, for some centuries now we have not failed to see happening somewhere, now in one place, now in another, while the cruel Turks invade some parts of the Christian dominion and other parts are torn asunder by the internal strife of manifold heretical sects.

Whenever we see such things or hear that they are beginning to happen, however far away, let us think that this is no time for us to sit and sleep but rather to get up immediately and bring relief to the danger of others in whatever way we can—by our prayers at least, if in no other way. Nor is such danger to be taken lightly because it happens at some distance from us. Certainly if that saying of the comic poet [Terence] is so highly approved, "Since I am a man, I consider nothing human to be foreign to me," how could it be anything but disgraceful for Christians to snore while other Christians are in danger? In order to suggest this, Christ directed His warning to watch and pray not only to those He had placed nearby but also to those He had caused to remain at some distance. Then too, if we are perhaps unmoved by the misfortunes of others because they are at some distance from us, let us at least be moved by our own danger. For we have reason to fear that the destructive force will make its way from them to us, taught as we are by many examples how rapid the rushing force of a blaze can be and how terrible the contagion of a spreading plague. Since, therefore, all human safeguards are useless without the help of God to ward off evils, let us always remember these words from the gospel and let us always imagine that Christ Himself is again addressing to us over and over those words of His: "Why are you sleeping? Get up and pray that you may not enter into temptation."

At this juncture another point occurs to us: that Christ is also betrayed into the hands of sinners when His most holy body in the sacrament is consecrated and handled by unchaste, profligate, and sacrilegious priests. When we see such things happen (and they happen only too often, alas), let us imagine that Christ Himself again says to us, "Why are you sleeping? Stay awake, get up, and pray that you may not enter into temptation, for the Son of Man is betrayed into the hands of sinners." From the example of bad priests the contamination of vice spreads easily among the people. And the less suitable for obtaining grace those persons are whose duty it is to watch and pray for the people, the more necessary it is for the people to stay awake, get up, and pray all the more earnestly for themselves—and not only for themselves but also for priests of this sort. For it will be much to the advantage of the people if bad priests improve.

Finally, Christ is betrayed into the hands of sinners in a special way among those of a certain sect: these people, though they receive the venerable sacrament of the

Eucharist more frequently and wish to give the impression of honoring it more piously by receiving it under both species (contrary to public custom, without any necessity, but not without a great affront to the Catholic Church), nevertheless these people blaspheme against what they have received under a show of honor, some of them by calling it true bread and true wine, some of them—and this is far worse—by calling it not only true but also mere bread and wine. For they altogether deny that the real body of Christ is contained in the sacrament, though they call it by that name ["corpus Christi"]. When at this late date they set out to do such a thing, against the most open passages of Scripture, against the clearest interpretations of all the saints, against the most constant faith of the whole Church for so many centuries, against the truth most amply witnessed to by so many thousands of miracles— this group that labors under the second kind of infidelity (by far the worse), how little difference is there, I ask you, between them and those who took Christ captive that night? How little difference between them and those troops of Pilate who in jest bent their knees before Christ as if they were honoring Him while they insulted Him and called Him the king of the Jews, just as these people kneel before the Eucharist and call it the body of Christ—which according to their own profession they no more believe than the soldiers of Pilate believed Christ was a king. Therefore, whenever we hear that such evils have befallen other peoples, no matter how distant, let us immediately imagine that Christ is urgently addressing us: "Why are you sleeping? Get up and pray that you may not enter into temptation." For the fact is that wherever this plague rages today most fiercely, everyone did not catch the disease in a single day. Rather the contagion spreads gradually and imperceptibly while those persons who despise it at first, afterwards can stand to hear it and respond to it with less than full scorn, then come to tolerate wicked discussions, and afterwards are carried away into error, until like a cancer (as the apostle says) the creeping disease finally takes over the whole country [2 Tm 2:17]. Therefore let us stay awake, get up, and pray continually that all those who have fallen into this miserable folly through the wiles of Satan may quickly come to their senses and that God may never suffer us to enter into this kind of temptation and may never allow the devil to roll the blasts of this storm of his to our shores. But so much for my digression into these mysteries; let us now return to the historical events.

Judas, therefore, when he had received a cohort from the chief priests and servants from the Pharisees, came there with lanterns and torches. [Jn 18:3] And while Jesus was still speaking, behold, Judas Iscariot, one of the twelve, and with him a large crowd with swords and clubs, sent by the chief priests and scribes and elders of the people. The traitor, however, had given them a sign.... [Mt 26:47-48, Mk 14:43-44]

I tend to believe that the cohort which according to the accounts of the evangelists was handed over to the traitor by the high priests was a Roman cohort assigned to the high priests by Pilate. To it the Pharisees, scribes, and elders of the people had added their own servants, either because they did not have enough confidence in the governor's soldiers or because they thought extra numbers would help prevent Christ from being rescued through some sudden confusion caused by the darkness, or perhaps for another reason—their desire to arrest at the same time all the apostles, without letting any of them escape in the dark. They were prevented from executing this part of their plan by the power of Christ Himself, who was Himself captured only because He, and He alone, wished to be taken.

They carry smoking torches and dim lanterns so that they might be able to discern through the darkness of sin the bright sun of justice, not that they might be enlightened by the light of Him who enlightens every man that comes into this world, but that they might put out that eternal light of His which can never be darkened. And like master like servant, for those who sent them strove to overthrow the law of God for the sake of their traditions. Even now some still follow in their footsteps and persecute Christ by striving mightily to overshadow the splendor of God's glory for the sake of their own glory. But in this passage it is worthwhile to pay close attention to the constant revolutions and vicissitudes of the human condition. For not six days before, even the gentiles had been eager to get a look at Christ, because of His remarkable miracles together with the great holiness of His life [Jn 12:20-22]. But the Jews had welcomed Him with truly extraordinary reverence as He rode into Jerusalem. But now the Jews, joining forces with the gentiles, come to arrest Him like a thief; and not merely among them but at their head was a man worse than all the gentiles and Jews put together, Judas. Thus in His death Christ took care to provide this contrast as a notable warning to all men that no one should expect blind Fortune to stand still for him, and that no Christian especially, as one who hopes for heaven, should pursue the contemptible glory of this world.

The persons responsible for sending the crowd after Christ were priests—and not merely that, but princes of the priests—Pharisees, scribes, and elders of the people. Here we see that whatever is best by nature turns out in the end to be the worst, once it begins to reverse its direction. Thus Lucifer, created by God as the most eminent among the angels in heaven, became the worst of the demons after he yielded to the pride which brought his downfall. So too, not the dregs of the crowd but the elders of the people, the scribes, Pharisees, priests, and high priests, the princes of the priests, whose duty it was to see that justice was done and to promote the affairs of God, these were the very ringleaders in a conspiracy to extinguish the sun of justice and to destroy the only-begotten son of God—to such insane extremes of perversity were they driven by avarice, arrogance, and envy.

Another point should not be passed over lightly but should be given careful consideration: Judas, who in many other places is called by the infamous name "traitor," is here also disgraced by the lofty title "apostle." "Behold," he says, "Judas Iscariot, one of the twelve"—Judas Iscariot, who was not one of the unbelieving pagans, not one of the Jewish enemies, not one of Christ's ordinary disciples (and even that would have been incredible enough), but (O the shame of it!) one of Christ's chosen apostles—can bear to hand over his Lord to be captured, and even to be the leader of the captors himself.

There is in this passage a lesson to be learned by all who exercise high public office: when they are addressed with solemn titles, they do not always have reason to be proud and congratulate themselves; rather, such titles are truly fitting only if those who bear them know in their hearts that they have in fact lived up to such honorific names by conscientiously performing their duties. For otherwise they may very well be overcome with shame (unless they find pleasure in the empty jingle of words), since wicked men in high office—whether they be great men, princes, great lords, emperors, priests, bishops, it makes no difference as long as they are wicked—certainly ought to realize that whenever men titillate their ears by crooning their splendid titles of office, they do not do so sincerely, in order to pay them true honor, but rather to reproach them freely by seeming to praise those honors which they bear in so unpraiseworthy a fashion. So too in the Gospel, when Judas is celebrated under his title of apostle in the phrase "Judas Iscariot, one of the twelve," the real intent is anything but praise, as is clear from the fact that in the next breath he is called a traitor. "For the traitor," according to the account, "had given them a signal, saying, 'Whomever I kiss, that is the one. Seize him'."

At this point the usual question is why it was necessary for the traitor to give the crowd a signal identifying Jesus. To this, some answer that they agreed on a signal because more than once before, Christ had suddenly escaped from the hands of those who were trying to apprehend Him. But since this usually happened in the daytime, when He was escaping from the hands of those who already recognized Him, and since He did it by employing His divine power, either to disappear from their sight or to pass from their midst while they were in a state of shock, against this sort of escape giving a signal to identify Him could not be of any use.

And so others say that one of the two Jameses looked very much like Christ—and for that reason, they think, he was called the brother of Christ [Gal 1:19]—so much so that unless you looked at them closely you could not tell them apart. But since they could have arrested both of them and taken both away with them to be identified later at their leisure by comparing them at close quarters, what need was there to worry about a signal?

The Gospel makes it clear that the night was far advanced; and although daybreak was drawing near, it was still nighttime and quite dark, as is evident from the torches and lanterns they carried, which gave enough light to make them visible from some distance but hardly enough for them to discern anyone else from afar. And although on that night they perhaps had the advantage of some faint light from the full moon, it could only have been enough to make out the shapes of bodies in the distance, not to get a good view of facial features and distinguish one person from another. Hence if they went rushing in at random in the hope of capturing all of them at once, each man choosing his victim without knowing who he was, they were afraid, and rightly so, that out of so many some (by all odds) might perhaps get away and that one of the fugitives might well be the very man they had come for. For those who are in the greatest danger are likely to be the quickest to look out for themselves.

Thus, whether they thought of this or whether Judas himself suggested it, they set their trap by having the betrayer go on ahead to single out the Lord by embracing and kissing Him. In this way, when they had all fixed their eyes on Him alone, each and every one of them could try to get his hands on Him. After that, if any of the others got away it would not be such a dangerous matter. "Therefore the traitor had given them a signal, saying, 'Whomever I kiss, that is the one. Seize him and take him away carefully'."

O the lengths to which greed will go! Couldn't you be satisfied, you treacherous scoundrel, with betraying your Lord (who had raised you to the lofty office of an apostle) into the hands of impious men by the signal of a kiss, without also being so concerned that He should be taken away carefully, lest He might escape from His captors? You were hired to betray Him; others were sent to take him, to guard Him, to produce Him in court. But you, as if your role in the crime were not important enough, go on to meddle in the duties of the soldiers; and as if the villainous magistrates who sent them had not given them adequate instructions, there was a need for a circumspect man like you to add your own gratuitous cautions and commands that they must lead Him away carefully once He is captured. Were you afraid that even though you had fully performed your criminal task by betraying Christ to His assassins, still if the soldiers had somehow been so remiss that Christ escaped through their carelessness or was rescued by force against their will—were you afraid that then your thirty pieces of silver, that illustrious reward of your heinous crime, would not be paid? Have no fear, they will be paid. But believe me, you are no more eager and greedy to get them now than you will be impatient and anxious to throw them away once you have gotten them. Meanwhile you will go on to complete a deed that brings pain to your Lord and death to you, but salvation to many.

He went ahead of them and came up to Jesus to kiss Him. And when he had come, he went right up to Him and said, "Rabbi, hail Rabbi," and he kissed Him. Jesus said to him, "Friend, why have you come?" [Mt 26:49-50] "Judas, are you betraying the Son of Man with a kiss?" [Lk 22:48]
Though Judas really did, as a matter of historical fact, precede the crowd, still this also means in a spiritual sense that among those who share in the same sinful act, the one who has most reason to abstain takes precedence in God's judgment of their guilt.

"And he came up to Him to kiss Him. And when he had come, he went right up to Him and said, 'Rabbi, hail Rabbi.' And he kissed Him." In this same way Christ is approached, greeted, called "Rabbi," kissed, by those who pretend to be disciples of Christ, professing His teaching in name but striving in fact to undermine it by crafty tricks and stratagems. In just this way Christ is greeted as "Rabbi" by anyone who calls Him master and scorns His precepts. In just this way is He kissed by those priests who consecrate the most holy body of Christ and then put to death Christ's members, Christian souls, by their false teaching and wicked example. In just this way is Christ greeted and kissed by those who demand to be considered good and pious because at the persuasion of bad priests they, though laymen, receive the sacred body and blood of Christ under both species, without any real need for it but not without great contempt for the whole Catholic Church and therefore not without grave sin. And this these latter-day saints do against the long-standing practice and custom of all Christians. And not only do they themselves do it (that we could somehow manage to put up with), but they condemn everyone who receives both substances under only one of the two species—that is, apart from themselves, all Christians everywhere for these many years. And still, though they hotly insist that both species are necessary for the laity, most of them—both laymen and priests—eliminate the reality, that is, the body and blood, from both species, keeping only the words "body" and "blood." In this respect, indeed, they are not unlike Pilate's guards, who mocked Christ by kneeling before Him and saluting Him as the king of the Jews. For these men likewise genuflect in veneration of the Eucharist and call it the body and blood of Christ though they no more believe it is the one or the other than the soldiers of Pilate believed Christ was a king.

Now all these groups which I have enumerated certainly bring to our minds the traitor Judas, in that they combine a greeting and a kiss with treachery. But just as they renew an action of the past, so Joab (2 Sam 20) once provided a prophetic figure of the future: for "when he had greeted Amasa thus, 'Greetings, my brother,' and had caressed Amasa's chin with his right hand" as if he were about to kiss him, he stealthily unsheathed a hidden sword and killed him with one stroke through his side, and by a similar trick he had formerly killed Abner; but later (as was only right) he justly paid with his life for his heinous deception. Judas rightly calls to mind and represents Joab, whether you consider the status of the persons involved or the deceitful treachery of the crime or the vengeance of

God and the bad end both came to—with this difference, that Judas surpassed Joab in every respect.

Joab enjoyed great favor and influence with his prince; Judas had even more with an even greater prince. Joab killed Amasa, who was his friend; Judas killed Jesus, who was an even closer friend, not to say also his Lord. Joab was motivated by envy and ambition because he had heard that the king would promote Amasa above him; but Judas, enticed by greed for a miserable reward, for a few pieces of silver, betrayed the Lord of the world to His death. In the same degree, therefore, as Judas' crime was worse, the vengeance exacted from him was the more devastating. For Joab was killed by another, but the most wretched Judas hanged himself with his own hand.

But in the treacherous pattern of their deception, there is a nice equivalence between the crimes of Joab and Judas. For just as Joab kills Amasa in the very act of courteously greeting him and preparing to kiss him, so too Judas approaches Christ affably, greets Him reverently, kisses Him lovingly, and all the time the villainous wretch has nothing else in mind than to betray his Lord to His death. But Joab was able to deceive Amasa by flattery; not so Judas with Christ. He receives his advances, listens to his greeting, does not refuse his kiss; and though aware of his abominable treachery, He nevertheless acted for a while as if He were completely ignorant of everything. Why did He do this? Was it to teach us to feign and dissemble and with polite cunning to turn the deception back upon the deceiver? Hardly, but rather to teach us to bear patiently and gently all injuries and snares treacherously set for us; not to smolder with anger, not to seek revenge, not to give vent to our feelings by hurling back insults, not to find an empty pleasure in tripping up an enemy through some clever trick, but rather to set ourselves against deceitful injury with genuine courage, to conquer evil with good—

in fine, to make every effort by words both gentle and harsh, to insist both in season and out of season, that the wicked may change their ways to good, so that if anyone should be suffering from a disease that does not respond to treatment, he may not blame the failure on our negligence but rather attribute it to the virulence of his own disease. And so Christ as a most conscientious physician tries both ways of effecting a cure. Employing first of all gentle words, He says, "Friend, why have you come?"

When he heard himself called "friend," the traitor was left hanging in doubt. For since he was aware of his own crime, he was afraid that Christ used the title "friend" as a severe rebuke for his hostile unfriendliness. On the other hand, since criminals always flatter themselves with the hope that their crimes are unknown, he was blind and mad enough to hope (even though he had often learned by personal experience that the thoughts of men lay open to Christ, and though his own treachery had been touched upon at the [last] supper), nevertheless, I say, he was so demented and oblivious to everything as to hope that his villainous deed had escaped Christ's notice.

But because nothing could be more unwholesome for him than to be duped by such a futile hope (for nothing could work more strongly against his repentance than this), Christ in His goodness no longer allows him to be led on by a deceptive hope of deceiving but immediately adds in a grave tone, "Judas, do you betray the Son of Man with a kiss?" He addresses him by the name He had ordinarily used—and for this reason, so that the memory of their old friendship might soften the heart of the traitor and move him to repent. He openly rebukes his treachery lest he should believe it is hidden and be ashamed to confess it. Moreover, He reviles the impious hypocrisy of the traitor: "With a kiss," He says, "do you betray the Son of Man?"

Among all the circumstances of a wicked deed it is not

easy to find one more hateful to God than the perversion of the real nature of good things to make them into the instruments of our malice. Thus lying is hateful to God because words, which are ordained to express the meaning of the mind, are twisted to other, deceitful purposes. Within this category of evil, it is a serious offense against God if anyone abuses the law to inflict the very injuries it was designed to prevent. And so Christ reproaches Judas sharply for this detestable kind of sin: "Judas," He says, "do you betray the Son of Man with a kiss? Either be in fact as you wish to seem or else show yourself openly as you really are. For whoever commits such an unfriendly misdeed under the guise of a friend is a villain who compounds his villainy. Were you not satisfied, Judas, with betraying the Son of Man—indeed, I say, the son of that man through whom all men would have perished if this Son of Man, whom you imagine you are destroying, had not redeemed those who wish to be saved—was it not enough for you, I say, to betray this Son of Man without doing it with a kiss, thus turning the most sacred sign of charity into an instrument of betrayal? Certainly I am more favorably disposed toward this mob which attacks me with open force than toward you, Judas, who betray me to the attackers with a false kiss."

And so when Christ saw no sign of repentance in the traitor, wishing to show how much more willing He was to speak with open enemies than with a secret foe, having made it clear to the traitor that He cared not a whit for all his wicked stratagems, He immediately turned away from him and made His way, unarmed as He was, toward the armed crowd. For so the Gospel says: "And then Jesus, knowing everything that was to happen to Him, went forward and said to them, 'Whom do you seek?' They replied to Him, 'Jesus of Nazareth.' Jesus said to them, 'I am He.' Now Judas, who betrayed Him, was also standing with them. When, therefore, He said to them, 'I am He,' they drew back and fell to the ground."

O saving Christ, only a little while ago you were so fearful that you lay face down in a most pitiable attitude and sweat blood as you begged your Father to take away the chalice of your passion. How is it that now, by a sudden reversal, you leap up and spring forth like a giant running his race and come forward eagerly to meet those who seek to inflict that passion upon you? How is it that you freely identify yourself to those who openly admit they are seeking you but who do not know that you are the one they are seeking? Hither, hither let all hasten who are faint of heart. Here let them take firm hold of an unwavering hope when they feel themselves struck by a horror of death. For just as they share Christ's agony, His fear, grief, anxiety, sadness, and sweat (provided that they pray, and persist in prayer, and submit themselves wholeheartedly to the will of God), they will also share this consolation. Undoubtedly they will feel themselves helped by such consolation as Christ felt, and they will be so refreshed by the spirit of Christ that they will feel their hearts renewed as the old face of the earth is renewed by the dew from heaven; and by means of the wood of Christ's cross let down into the water of their sorrow, the thought of death, once so bitter, will grow sweet, eagerness will take the place of grief, mental strength and courage will replace dread, and finally they will long for the death they had viewed with horror, considering life a sad thing and death a gain, desiring to be dissolved and to be with Christ.

"And so Christ, coming up close to the crowd, asks, 'Whom do you seek?' They replied to Him, 'Jesus of Nazareth.' Now Judas, who betrayed Him, was standing with them. And Jesus said to them, 'I am He.' When, therefore, Jesus said to them, 'I am He,' they drew back and fell to the ground." If Christ's previous fear and anxiety lessened His standing in anyone's mind, the balance must now be redressed by the manly courage with which He fearlessly approaches that whole mass of armed men and, though He faces certain death ("for He knew everything which was to happen to Him"), betrays Himself by His own act to those villains, who did not even know who He was, and thus offers Himself freely as a victim to be cruelly slaughtered.

Certainly this sudden and drastic change would rightly be considered marvelous viewed simply as occurring in His venerable human nature. But what sort of estimate of Him, how intense a reaction to Him must be produced in the hearts of all the faithful by the force of divine power flashing so wonderfully through the weak body of a man? For how was it that none of His pursuers recognized Him when He came up close to them? He had taught in the temple. He had overturned the tables of the money-changers. He had driven out the money-changers themselves. He had carried out His activities in public. He had confuted the Pharisees, He had satisfied the Sadducees [Mt 22:23-33], He had refuted the scribes, He had eluded by a prudent answer the trick question of the Herodian soldiers [Mt 22:15-22]. He had fed seven thousand men with five loaves, He had healed the sick, raised the dead, made Himself available to all sorts of men—Pharisees, tax-gatherers, the rich, the poor, just men, sinners, Jews, Samaritans, and gentiles. And now in this whole large crowd there was no one who recognized Him by His face or voice as He addressed them near at hand, as if those who sent them had taken special care not to send anyone along who had ever seen beforehand the person they were then seeking.

Had no one even singled out Christ from His meeting with Judas, from the embrace and the sign Judas gave with a kiss? Even more, the traitor himself, who was at that time standing together with them, did he suddenly forget how to recognize the very person he had just betrayed by singling Him out with a kiss? What was the source of this strange happening? Indeed, no one was able to recognize Him for the very same reason that a little later Mary Magdalen, though she saw Him, did not recognize Him until He revealed Himself, and likewise neither one of the two disciples, though they were talking with Him, knew who He was until He let them know, but rather the two disciples thought He was a traveler and she thought He was a gardener. Finally, then, if you want to know how it was that no one could recognize Him when He came up to them, you should undoubtedly attribute it to the same cause you use to explain the fact that when He spoke no one could remain standing: "But when Jesus said, 'I am He,' they drew back and fell to the ground."

Here Christ proved that He truly is that word of God which pierces more sharply than any two-edged sword. Thus a lightning bolt is said to be of such a nature that it liquefies a sword without damaging the sheath. Certainly the mere voice of Christ, without damaging their bodies, so melted their souls that it deprived them of the strength to hold up their limbs.

Here the evangelist relates that Judas was standing together with them. For when he heard Jesus rebuke him openly as a traitor, whether overcome with shame or struck with fear (for he was acquainted with Peter's impulsiveness), he immediately withdrew and returned to his own kind. Thus the evangelist tells us he was standing together with them so that we may understand that like them he also fell down. And certainly the character of Judas was such that there was in that whole crowd no one worse or more worthy of being cast down. But the evangelist wished to impress upon everyone generally that they must be careful and cautious about the company they keep, for there is a danger that if they take their place with wicked men they will also fall together with them. It rarely happens that a person who is foolish enough to cast his lot with those who are headed for shipwreck in an unseaworthy vessel gets back to land alive after the others have drowned in the sea.

No one, I suppose, doubts that a person who could throw them all down with one word could easily have dashed them all down so forcibly that none of them could have gotten back up again. But Christ, who struck them down to let them know that they could inflict no suffering upon Him against His will, allowed them to get up again so that they could accomplish what He wished to endure: "And so when they had gotten up, He asked them once more, 'Whom do you seek?' And they said to Him, 'Jesus of Nazareth'."

Here too, anyone can see that they were so daunted, stunned, and stupefied by their meeting with Christ that they seem almost to be out of their minds. For they might very well have known that at that time of night and in that place they would not find anyone who was not one of Christ's band of followers or else a friend of His, and that the last thing in the world such a person would do would be to lead them to Christ. And yet, suddenly meeting a person whose identity was unknown to them as well as the reason for His question, right away they foolishly blurt out the heart of the whole affair, which they ought to have kept carefully concealed until they had carried it out. For as soon as He asked, "Whom do you seek?" they replied, "Jesus of Nazareth." Jesus answered, "I have told you I am He. If, therefore, you seek me, let these men go their way"—as if to say: "If you are looking for me, now that I have approached you and let you know who I am by my own admission, why do you not arrest me on the spot? Surely the reason is that you are so far from being able to take me against my will that you cannot even remain standing at my mere words, as you have just learned by falling backwards. But now, if you have forgotten it so quickly, I again remind you that I am Jesus of Nazareth. If, therefore, you seek me, let these men go their way."

By throwing them down, Christ made it very clear, I think, that His words "Let these men go their way" did not constitute a request. But sometimes it happens that those who are planning some great piece of villainy are not content with the bare crime alone but with perverse wantonness make a practice of adding certain trimmings, as it were, beyond what is required by the scope of the crime itself. Moreover, there are some ministers of crime who are so preposterously faithful that to avoid the risk of omitting any evil deed that has been entrusted to them, they will add something extra on their own for good measure. Christ implicitly refers to each of these two types. "If you seek me," He says, "let these go their way": "If my blood is what the chief priests, the scribes, Pharisees, and elders of the people are longing to drain away with such an eager thirst, behold, when you were seeking me, I came to meet you; when you did not know me, I betrayed myself to you; when you were prostrate, I stood nearby; now that you are arising, I stand ready to be taken captive; and finally, I myself hand myself over to you (which the traitor was not able to do) to keep my followers and you from imagining (as if it were not crime enough to kill me) that their blood must be added over and above mine. Therefore, if you seek me, let these men go their way."

He commanded them to let them go, but He also forced them to do so against their will, and by seeing to it that all were saved by flight He frustrated their efforts to capture them. An indication of this outcome was what He intended by this prophetic statement of His, "Let these men go their way," so that those words He had spoken might be fulfilled: "Of those you have given me, I have not lost anyone" [Jn 18:9]. The words of Christ which the evangelist is talking about here are those words He spoke to His Father that same night at supper: "Holy Father, preserve in your name those whom you have given to me." And afterwards: "I have guarded those whom you gave to me, and none of them has perished except the son of perdition, that the Scripture might be fulfilled." See how Christ here, as He foretells that the disciples will be saved when He is taken captive, declares that He is their guardian. Hence the evangelist recalls this to the minds of his readers, wishing them to understand that in spite of His words to the crowd, "Let these men go their way," He Himself by His hidden power had opened up a way for their escape.

The place in Scripture which predicts that Judas would perish is in Psalm 109, where the psalmist prophesies in the form of a prayer: "May his days be few, and may another take over his ministry" [Ps 109:8]. Although these prophetic words were spoken about the traitor Judas such a long time before the event, nevertheless it would be hard to say whether anyone apart from the psalmist himself knew that they referred to Judas until Christ made this clear and the event itself bore out the words. Even the prophets themselves did not see everything foreseen by other prophets. For the spirit of prophecy is measured out individually. Certainly it seems clear to me that no one understands the meaning of all scriptural passages so well that there are not many mysteries hidden there which are not yet understood, whether concerning the times of the Antichrist or the last judgment by Christ, and which will remain unknown until Elijah returns to explain them [Mal 3:23]. Therefore it seems to me that I can justly apply the apostle's exclamation about God's wisdom to holy Scripture (in which God has hidden and laid up the vast stores of His wisdom): "O the depth of the riches of the wisdom and knowledge of God! How incomprehensible are His judgments and how unsearchable His ways!" [Rom 11:33].

And nevertheless nowadays, first in one place, then in another, there are springing up from day to day, almost like swarms of wasps or hornets, people who boast that they are "autodidacts" (to use St. Jerome's word) and that, without the commentaries of the old doctors, they find clear, open, and easy all those things which all the ancient Fathers confessed they found quite difficult—and the Fathers were men of no less talent or training, of tireless energy, and as for that "spirit" which these moderns have as often on their lips as they do rarely in their hearts, here the Fathers surpassed them no less than in holiness of life. But now these modern men who have sprouted up overnight as theologians professing to know everything not only disagree about the meaning of Scripture with all those men who led such heavenly lives, but also fail to agree among themselves concerning great dogmas of the Christian faith. Rather, each of them, whoever he may be, insisting that he sees the truth, conquers the rest and is in turn conquered by them. But they all are alike in opposing the Catholic faith, and all are alike in being conquered by it. He who dwells in the heavens laughs to scorn these wicked and vain attempts of theirs [Ps 2:4]. But I humbly pray that He may not so laugh them to scorn as to laugh also at their eternal ruination, but rather that He may inspire in them the health-giving grace of repentance, so that these prodigal sons who have wandered so long, alas, in exile may retrace their steps to the bosom of Mother Church, and so that all of us together, united in the true faith of Christ and joined in mutual charity as true members of Christ, may attain to the glory of Christ our head, which no one should ever be foolish enough to hope to arrive at outside the body of Christ and without the true faith.

But to return to what I was saying, the fact that this prophetic utterance applies to Judas was suggested by

Christ [Jn 17:12], was made clear by Judas' suicide, was afterwards made quite explicit by Peter [Acts 1:20], and was fulfilled by all the apostles when Matthias was chosen by lot to take his place [Acts 1:26] and thus another took over his ministry. And to make the matter even clearer, after Matthias took Judas' place no replacement was ever taken into that group of twelve (although bishops succeed in the place of the apostles in an uninterrupted line), but rather, as the apostleship was transmitted gradually to more persons, that sacred number came to an end once the prophecy had been fulfilled.

Therefore, when Christ said, "Let these men go their way," He was not begging for their permission but rather declaring in veiled terms that He Himself granted His disciples the power to leave, that He might fulfill those words He had spoken: "Father, I have guarded those whom you gave to me, and none of them has perished except the son of perdition." I think it worthwhile to consider here for a moment how strongly Christ foretold in these words the contrast between the end of Judas and the end of the rest, the ruination of the traitor Judas and the success of the others. For He asserts each future outcome with such certainty that He announces them not as future happenings but as events that have already definitely taken place. "I have guarded," He says, "those whom you gave to me." They were not defended by their own strength, nor were they preserved by the mercy of the Jews, nor did they escape through the carelessness of the cohort, but rather "I guarded them. And none of them perished except the son of perdition": "For he too, Father, was among those whom you gave to me. Chosen by me, he received me, and to him as well as to the rest who received me I had given the power to become a son of God. But when in his insane greed he went over to Satan, leaving me, betraying me treacherously, refusing to be saved, then he became a son of destruction in the very act of pursuing my destruction, and perished like a wretch in his wretchedness."

Infallibly certain about the fate of the traitor, Christ expresses his future ruin with such certainty that He asserts it as if it had already come to pass. And for all that, as Christ is being arrested, the unhappy traitor stands there as the ferocious leader and standard-bearer of Christ's captors, rejoicing and exulting, I imagine, in the danger of his fellow-disciples and his master, for I am convinced he desired and hoped that all of them would be arrested and put to death. The raving madness and perversity of ingratitude manifests itself in this peculiarity: the ingrate desires the death of the very victim he has unjustly injured. So too, the person whose conscience is full of guilty sores is so sensitive that he views even the face of his victim as a reproach and shrinks from it with dread. Thus as the traitor rejoiced in the hope that all of them would be captured together, he was so stupidly sure of himself that nothing was further from his mind than the thought that the death sentence passed on him by God was hanging over his head like a dreadful noose ready to fall around his neck at any moment.

In this connection I am struck by the lamentable obscurity of the miserable human condition: often we are distressed and fearful, ignorant all the while that we are quite safe; often, on the other hand, we act as if we had not a care in the world, unaware that the death-dealing sword hangs over our heads. The other apostles were afraid they would be seized together with Christ and put to death, whereas actually they were all to escape. Judas, who had no fears for himself and took pleasure in their fears, perished only a few hours later. Cruel is the appetite which feeds on the misery of others. Nor is there any reason why a person should rejoice and congratulate himself on his good fortune because he has it in his power to cause another man's death, as the traitor thought he had by means of the cohort that had been delivered to him. For though a man may send someone else to his death, he himself is sure to follow him there. Even more, since the hour of death is uncertain, he himself may precede the very person he arrogantly imagines he has sent to death ahead of him.

Thus the death of the wretched Judas preceded that of Christ, whom he had betrayed to His death—a sad and terrible example to the whole world that the wrongdoer, however he may flout his arrogant impenitence, ought not to think he is safe from retribution. For against the wicked all creatures work together in harmony with their Creator [Ws 5:21-24, 16:16-17]. The air longs to blow noxious vapors against the wicked man, the sea longs to overwhelm him in its waves, the mountains to fall upon him, the valleys to rise up against him, the earth to split open beneath him, hell to swallow him up after his headlong fall, the demons to plunge him into gulfs of ever-burning flames. All the while the only one who preserves the wretch is the God whom he deserted.

But if anyone is such a persistent imitator of Judas that God finally decides not to offer any longer the grace which has been offered and refused so often, this man is really and truly wretched: however he may flatter himself in the delusion that he is floating high in the air on the wings of felicity, he is actually wallowing in the utter depths of misery and calamity. Therefore let each of us pray to the most merciful Christ, each praying not only for himself but also for others, that we may not imitate Judas in his stubbornness but rather may eagerly accept the grace God offers us and may be restored once more to glory through penance and mercy.

The Severing of Malchus' Ear, the Flight of the Apostles, and the Capture of Christ

The Severing of Malchus' Ear

The apostles had previously heard Christ foretelling the very things they were now seeing happen. On that occasion, though they were saddened and grieved, they treated the matter with much less concern than now when they see it happening before their very eyes. Now that they see the whole cohort standing there and openly admitting that they are seeking Jesus of Nazareth, there is no more room for doubt that they are seeking Him to take Him captive.

When the apostles saw what was about to happen, their minds were overwhelmed by a sudden welter of different feelings: anxiety for their Lord whom they loved, fear for their own safety, and finally shame for that high-sounding promise of theirs that they would all rather die than fail their Master. Thus their impulses were divided between conflicting feelings. Their love of their Master urged them not to flee; their fear for themselves, not to remain. Fear of death impelled them to run away; shame for their promise, to stand fast.

Moreover, they remembered what Christ had said to them that very night: He told them that whereas before He had forbidden any of them to carry so much as a staff to defend himself with [Mt 10:10], now whoever did not have a sword should even sell his tunic to buy one. Now they were struck with great fear as they saw massed against them the Roman cohort and the crowd of Jews, all of them armed with weapons, whereas there were only eleven of them, and even of those none had any weapons (apart perhaps from table knives), except two who had swords. Nevertheless, they remembered that when they had said to Christ, "Look, here are two swords," He had replied, "That is enough." Not understanding the great mystery contained in this reply, they suddenly and impulsively ask Him whether He wants them to defend Him with the sword, saying, "Lord, shall we strike with the sword?"

But Peter's feelings boiled over so that he did not wait for a reply but drew his sword, struck a blow at the servant of the high priest, and cut off his right ear—perhaps simply because this man happened to be standing next to Peter, perhaps because his fierce and haughty bearing made him conspicuous among the rest. At any rate, he certainly seems to have been a notoriously wicked man, for the evangelists mention that he was the servant of the high priest, the chief and prince of all the priests. "The greater the house, the prouder the servants," as the satirist [Juvenal] says, and men know from experience that everywhere in the world the servants of great lords are more arrogant and overbearing than their masters. That we might know that this man had some standing with the high priest and was for that reason all the more egregiously proud, John immediately adds his name: "The servant's name," he says, "was Malchus." The evangelist does not ordinarily provide such information everywhere or without some special reason.

I imagine that this rascal, displaying such fierceness as he thrust himself forward, irked Peter, who chose this enemy to open the fight and who would have pressed the attack vigorously if Christ had not checked his course. For Christ immediately forbade the others to fight, declared

Peter's zeal ineffectual, and restored the ear of this miserable creature. These things He did because He came to suffer death, not to escape it; and even if He had not come to die, He would not have needed such assistance. To make this more manifest, He first gave His reply to the question put by the other apostles: "Let them go this far." "Still give them leave for a while. For I cast them all down with a mere word, and yet even I, as you see, allowed them to get up so that for the present they may accomplish whatever they wish. Since, then, I allow them to go so far, you must do the same. The time will shortly come when I will no longer allow them any power against me. Even now, in the meantime, I do not need your help."

Thus to the others He answered only, "Let them go this far." But turning to Peter separately, He said, "Put your sword away"—as if to say: "I do not wish to be defended with the sword, and I have chosen you for the mission of fighting not with such a sword but with the sword of the word of God. Therefore return the sword of iron to the sheath where it belongs—that is, to the hands of worldly princes to be used against evildoers. You who are the apostles of my flock have yet another sword far more terrible than any sword of iron, a sword by which a wicked man is sometimes cut off from the Church (like a rotten limb removed from my mystical body) and handed over to Satan for the destruction of the flesh to save the spirit [1 Cor 5:5] (provided only that the man is of a mind to be healed) and to enable him once more to be joined and grafted into my body—though it sometimes happens that a man suffering from a hopeless disease is also handed over to the invisible death of the soul, lest he should infect the healthy members with his disease. But I am so far from wishing you to make use of that sword of iron (whose proper sheath, you must recognize, is the secular magistrate) that I do not think even that spiritual sword, whose use properly pertains to you, should be unsheathed very often. Rather, wield with vigor that sword of the word, whose stroke, like that of a scalpel, lets the pus out and heals by wounding. As for that other heavy and dangerous sword of excommunication, I desire that it be kept hidden in the sheath of mercy unless some urgent and fearful necessity requires that it be withdrawn."

In answering the other apostles Christ contented Himself with three words, because they were more temperate, or perhaps merely more tepid, than Peter; but Peter's fiery and wild assault He controlled and checked at greater length. He not only ordered him to put up his sword but also added the reason why He did not approve of his zeal, however pious. "Do you not wish me," He said, "to drink the chalice my Father gave me?" Some time ago Christ had predicted to the apostles that it would be "necessary for Him to go to Jerusalem and to suffer many things from the elders and scribes and princes of the priests, and to be killed, and to rise on the third day. And taking Him aside, Peter began to chide Him, saying, 'Far be it from you, O Lord. This will not happen to you.' Christ turned and said to Peter, 'Get behind me, Satan, for you do not understand the things of God'." Notice how severely Christ here rebuked Peter.

Shortly before, when Peter had professed that Christ was the son of God, Christ had said to him, "Blessed are you, Simon bar Jona, for flesh and blood have not revealed this to you, but rather my Father who is in heaven. And I say to you that you are Peter and upon this rock I will build my Church, and the gates of hell shall not prevail against it. And to you I will give the keys of heaven, and whatever you bind on earth will also be bound in heaven...." But here He almost rejects this same Peter and thrusts him behind Him and declares that he is a stumbling-block to Him and calls him Satan and asserts that he does not understand the things of God but rather those of men. And why does He do all this? Because Peter tried to persuade Him not to die. Then He showed that it was necessary for Him to follow through to His death, which was irrevocably decreed for Him by His own will; and hence not only did He not want them to hinder His death, He even wanted them to follow Him along the same road. "If anyone wishes to come after me," He said, "let him deny himself and take up his cross and follow me." Not satisfied even with this, He went on to show that if anyone refuses to follow Him on the road to death when the case requires it, he does not avoid death but incurs a much worse death; on the other hand, whoever gives up his life does not lose it but exchanges it for a more vital life. "Whoever wishes to save his life," He says, "will lose it. But whoever loses his life for my sake will find it. For what does it profit a man if he gain the whole world but suffer the loss of his own soul? Or what will a man give in exchange for his soul? For the Son of Man is to come with His angels in the glory of His Father, and then He will render to everyone according to his deeds."

Perhaps I have devoted more time to this passage [Mt 16:13-27] than was necessary. But I ask you, who would not be led beyond the pale, as they say, by these words of Christ, so severe and threatening but also so effective in creating hope of eternal life? But the relevance of these words to the passage under discussion is this: here we see Peter earnestly admonished not to be misled by his zeal into further hindering the death of Christ. And yet see now how Peter is again carried away by this same zeal to oppose Christ's death, except that this time he does not limit himself to verbal dissuasion but tries to ward it off by fierce fighting. Still, because Peter meant well when he did what he did, and also because Christ bore Himself with humility toward everyone as He drew near to His passion, Christ chose not to reprove Peter sharply. Rather, He first rebuked him by giving a reason, then He declared Peter's act to be sinful, and finally He announced that even if He wished to avoid death He would not need Peter's protection or any other mortal assistance, since if He wished help He had only to ask His Father, who would not fail to aid Him in His danger by sending a mighty and invincible array of angels against these puny mortals who were coming to take Him captive.

First of all, then, as I said, He checks Peter's zeal to strike out by presenting a rational argument. He says, "Do you not wish me to drink the chalice which my Father gave me?"—"My whole life up to this point has been a pattern of obedience and a model of humility. What lessons have I taught more frequently or more forcefully than that magistrates ought to be obeyed, that parents should be honored, that what is Caesar's should be rendered to Caesar, what is God's to God? And now, when I ought to be applying the finishing touches to bring my work to full perfection, now can you wish that I should refuse the chalice extended to me by my Father, that the Son of Man should disobey God the Father and thus unravel in a single moment all of that most beautiful fabric I have spent such a long time weaving?"

Then He teaches Peter that he committed a sin by striking with the sword, and this He does by a parallel from the civil law. "For everyone who takes up the sword," He says, "will perish by the sword." According to the Roman law, which also applied to the Jews at that time, any person discovered wearing a sword without legitimate authority, for the purpose of killing a man, was placed in almost the same category as the man who had killed his victim. Naturally, therefore, a person who not only wore a sword but also drew it and struck a blow was in even greater legal jeopardy. Nor do I think that Peter, in that moment of confusion and alarm, was so self-possessed that he deliberately avoided hitting Malchus' head and aimed only at his ear, so as merely to frighten him but not kill him.

But if someone should perhaps maintain that everyone has the right even to use force in order to protect an innocent person from criminal assault, this objection would require a longer discussion than I could conveniently introduce in this place. This much is certain: however much Peter's offense was mitigated by his loyal affection for Christ, nevertheless his lack of any legitimate authority to fight is made quite clear by the fact that on a previous occasion Christ had sharply warned him not to try to prevent His passion and death, not even by verbal dissuasion, much less by actual fighting.

Next He checks Peter's attack by making another point: Peter's protection is quite unnecessary. "Do you not know," He says, "that I could ask my Father for help and He would immediately deliver to me more than twelve legions of angels?"

About His own power He says nothing, but glories that He enjoys the favor of His Father. For as He drew near to His death, He wished to avoid lofty statements about Himself or any assertion that His own power was equal to that of the Father. Rather, wishing to make it clear that He had no need of help from Peter or any other mortal, He declares that the assistance of the heavenly angels (if He chose to ask for it) would immediately be at hand, sent by His omnipotent Father. "Do you not know," He says, "that I could ask my Father for help and He would immediately deliver to me more than twelve legions of angels?"—as if to say: "You have just seen before your very eyes how I threw down, with a mere word, without even touching them, this whole crowd, such a large crowd that it would be sheer folly for you to think you are strong enough to defend me against them. If that could not convince you that I do not need your help, consider at least whose son you proclaimed me to be when I put the question 'Who do you say I am?' and you immediately gave that heaven-inspired reply, 'You are Christ, the son of the living God.' Therefore, since you know from God's own revelation that I am the son of God, and since you must know that mortal parents do not fail their children, do you imagine that if I were not going to my death of my own free will, my heavenly Father would choose to fail me? Do you not know that if I chose to ask Him, He would deliver to me more than twelve legions of angels, and that He would do so forthwith, without hesitation or delay? Against so many legions of angels, what resistance could be offered by this miserable cohort of puny mortals? Ten times twelve legions of creatures such as these would not dare even to look upon the angry frown of a single angel."

Then Christ returns to His first point, as the one closest to the central issue. "How, then," He says, "will the Scriptures be fulfilled that say this is the way it must be?"

The Scriptures are full of prophecies concerning Christ's death, full of the mysteries of His passion and of mankind's redemption which would not have happened without that passion. Therefore, lest Peter or anyone else should mutter under his breath, "If you can obtain so many legions from your Father, Christ, why don't you ask for them?"—to counter this, Christ says, "How, then, will the Scriptures be fulfilled that say this is the way it must be?" "Since you understand from the Scriptures that this is the only way chosen by the most just wisdom of God to restore the human race to its lost glory, if I should now successfully implore my Father to save me from death, what would I be doing but striving to undo the very thing I came to do? To call down from heaven angels to defend me, what effect would that have but precisely to exclude from heaven the whole human race, which I come to redeem and restore to the glory of heaven? With your sword, therefore, you are not fighting against the wicked Jews but rather attacking the whole human race, inasmuch as you are setting yourself against the fulfillment of the Scriptures and desiring me not to drink the chalice given to me by my Father, that chalice by which I myself (unstained and undefiled) will wipe away that defiling stain of fallen nature."

But now behold the most gentle heart of Christ, who did not think it enough to check Peter's strokes but also touched the severed ear of His persecutor and made it sound again, in order to give us an example of rendering good for evil.

No one's body, I think, is so fully pervaded by his soul as the letter of holy Scripture is pervaded by spiritual mysteries. Indeed, just as one cannot touch any part of the body in which the soul does not reside, providing life and sensation to even the smallest part, so too no factual account in all of Scripture is so gross and corporeal (so to speak) that it does not have life and breath from some spiritual mystery. Therefore, in considering how Malchus' ear was cut off by Peter's sword and restored by the hand of Christ, we should not feel bound to consider only the facts of the account, though even these can teach us salutary lessons, but let us look further for the saving mystery of the spirit veiled beneath the letter of the story.

Thus Malchus, whose name is the Hebrew word for "king," can appropriately be taken as a figure of reason. For in man reason ought to reign like a king, and it does truly reign when it makes itself loyally subject to faith and serves God. For to serve Him is to reign. The high priest, on the other hand, together with his priests, with the Pharisees, scribes, and elders of the people, was given over to perverse superstitions which he mixed into the law of God, and he used piety as a pretext to oppose piety and sought eagerly to eliminate the founder of true religion. Hence he together with his accomplices may rightly be taken to represent wicked heresiarchs, the chief priests of pernicious superstition, together with their followers.

And so whenever the rational mind rebels against the true faith of Christ and devotes itself to heresies, it becomes a fugitive from Christ and a servant of the heresiarch whom it follows, led astray by the devil and wandering down the byways of error. Keeping, therefore, its left ear, with which it listens to sinister heresies, it loses its right ear, with which it ought to listen to the true faith. But this does not always happen from the same motivation or with the same effect. For some minds turn to heresies out of determined malice. Then the ear is not cut off by a swift stroke but rots slowly and gradually as the devil infuses his venom, until finally the purulent parts harden and block the passages with a clot so that nothing good can penetrate within. Such persons, alas, are hardly ever restored to health. For the parts eaten away by the ravaging cancer are completely gone and there is nothing left which can be put back in place.

But the ear cut off by a sudden stroke and sent whirling in one piece to the ground because of imprudent zeal stands for those who turn from the truth to a false appearance of the truth because they are overcome by a sudden impulse; or it also represents those who are deceived by a well-meaning zeal, concerning whom Christ says, "The time will come when everyone who kills you will think he is performing a service for God" [Jn 16:2]. Of this kind of person the apostle Paul was a typical figure. Some of these, because their minds are confused by earthly feelings, allow the ear which has been cut off from heavenly doctrine to remain lying on the earth. But Christ often takes pity on the misery of such persons and with His own hand picks up from the earth the ear which has been cut off by a sudden impulse or by ill-considered zeal and with His touch fastens it to the head again and makes it once more capable of listening to true doctrine. I know that the ancient Fathers elicited various mysteries from this one passage as each one, aided by the grace of the Holy Spirit, made his own particular discovery. But it is no part of my plan to review them all here, because to do so would make too long an interruption in the account of the historical events.

But Jesus said to those princes of the priests and magistrates of the temple and elders who had come, "You have come out with swords and clubs to seize me as if I were a robber, though I was with you every day in the temple, and I sat teaching there, and you did not detain me—you made no move to lay hands on me. But this is your hour and the power of darkness." [Lk 22:52-53, Mt 26:55, Mk 14:48-49]

Christ said this to those princes of the priests and magistrates of the temple and elders who had come. But here some readers are puzzled because the evangelist Luke reports that Jesus said these things to the princes of the priests and the magistrates of the temple and the elders of the people, while the other evangelists write in their accounts that these persons did not come themselves but sent the cohort and their servants.

Some solve the problem by saying that Jesus may indeed be said to have spoken to these persons because He spoke to those whom they had sent. In this sense princes ordinarily speak to one another through their ambassadors, and private persons everywhere speak to each other through messengers. Thus whatever we tell a servant who has been sent to us, we say to his master who sent him, for such servants will repeat to their master what they have been told.

Though I do not deny such a solution, I am certainly much more inclined to the opinion of those who think that Christ spoke face to face with the princes of the priests, magistrates of the temple, and elders of the people. For Luke does not say that Christ said these things to all the princes of the priests, or to all the magistrates of the temple, or to all the elders of the people, but only to those "who had come." These words seem to indicate rather clearly that although the cohort and servants had been commissioned to seize Christ in the name of the whole assembly gathered together in council, still some members of each group— elders, Pharisees, and princes—also went along with them. This opinion agrees exactly with Luke's words and does not contradict the accounts of the other evangelists.

Addressing, therefore, the princes of the priests, the Pharisees, and the elders of the people, Christ implicitly reminds them that they should not attribute His capture to their own strength or adroitness and should not foolishly boast of it as a clever and ingenious achievement (according to that unfortunate tendency of those who are fortunate in evil). He lets them know that the foolish contrivances and maneuvers by which they labored to suppress the truth were powerless to accomplish anything against Him, but rather the profound wisdom of God had foreseen and set the time when the prince of this world would be justly tricked into losing his ill-gotten prey, the human race, even as he strove by unjust means to keep it. If this were not the case, Christ explains to them, there would have been no need at all for them to pay for the services of the betrayer, to come at night with lanterns and torches, to make their approach surrounded by the dense ranks of the cohort and armed with swords and clubs, since they had previously had many opportunities to arrest Him as He sat teaching in the temple, and then they could have done it without expense, without any special effort, without spending a sleepless night, without any saber-rattling at all.

But if they should take special credit for their prudent foresight and say that the arrest of Christ was no easy matter, as He claimed, but rather quite difficult because it necessarily brought with it the great danger of a popular uprising [Mt 21:46], this difficulty for the most part had arisen only recently, after the resurrection of Lazarus. Before that event, it had happened more than once that in spite of the people's great love of His virtues and their profound respect for Him, He had had to use His own power to escape from their midst. On those occasions anyone attempting to capture and kill Him would not have been in the least danger from the crowd but would have found them to be willing accomplices in crime. So unfailingly unreliable is the common herd, always ready at a moment's notice to take the wrong side. Finally, what happened a little later showed how easy it is to brush aside the people's favor toward a person and any fear that might arise from it; as soon as He was arrested, the people were no less furious at Him as they cried out, "Away with him! Crucify him!" than they had formerly been eager to honor Him when they cried, "Blessed is He who comes in the name of the Lord!" and "Hosanna in the highest!"

And so up to that time God had caused the would-be captors of Christ to imagine purely fictitious grounds for fear and to tremble with dread where there was no reason to be afraid. But now that the proper time had come for all men (all, that is, who truly desire it) to be redeemed by the bitter death of one man and be restored to the sweetness of eternal life, these puny creatures stupidly imagined that they had achieved by clever planning what as a matter of fact God in His omnipotent providence (without which not a sparrow falls to earth) had mercifully prescribed from all eternity. To show them how very wrong they were and to let them know that without His own consent the deceitfulness of the betrayer and their own cleverly-laid snares and the power of the Romans would have been utterly ineffectual, Christ said, "But this is your hour and the power of darkness." These words of Christ are grounded firmly by what the evangelist says: "But all this was done so that the writings of the prophets might be fulfilled."

Predictions of Christ's death are very frequent throughout the prophets: "He was led like a lamb to the slaughter, and His cry was not heard in the streets" [Is 53:7, Ps 44:11]; "They have pierced my hands and my feet" [Ps 22:16]; "I was struck with these blows in the home of those who loved me" [Zech 13:6]; "And He was reckoned among the wicked" [Is 53:12]; "Truly He bore our infirmities" [Is 53:4]; "By His bruises we have been healed" [Is 53:5]; "He has been brought to His death by the wickedness of my people" [Is 53:8, 12]. The prophets are full of very clear predictions of the death of Christ. In order that these might not remain unfulfilled, it was necessary that the matter depend not on human planning but rather on Him who foresaw and prearranged from all eternity what would happen (that is, on the Father of Christ and likewise on Christ Himself and on the Holy Spirit of both of them, for the actions of these three are always so harmoniously unified that there is no exterior act of any one of them that does not belong equally to all three). The most suitable times of fulfillment, then, were already foreseen and prescribed. Therefore, while the high priests and the princes of the priests, the scribes, Pharisees, and elders of the people—in short, all these accursed and wicked magistrates—were taking pride in their masterful plan for capturing Christ cleverly, they were nothing more than tools of God, eager in their ignorance, blind instruments of the most excellent and unchangeable will of almighty God, not only of the Father and the Holy Spirit but also of Christ Himself; thus foolish and blind with malice, they did great harm to themselves and great good to others, they inflicted a temporary death on Christ but contributed to a most happy life for the human race, and they enhanced the everlasting glory of Christ.

And so Christ said to them, "This is your hour and the power of darkness": "In the past, although you hated me intensely, although you longed to destroy me, although you could have done so at that time with less trouble (except that heavenly power prevented it), yet you did not detain me in the temple—you did not even make a single move to lay hands on me. Why was this? It was because the time and the hour had not yet come, the hour fixed not by the heavenly bodies, not by your cleverness, but rather by the unsearchable plan of my Father, to which I too had given my consent. Would you like to know when He did this? Not only as long ago as the times of Abraham, but from all eternity. For from all eternity, together with the Father, before Abraham came to be, I am.

"And so this is your hour and the power of darkness. This is the short hour allowed to you and the power granted to darkness, so that now in the dark you might do what you were not permitted to do in the daylight, flying in my face like winged creatures from the Stygian marsh, like harpies, like horned owls and screech-owls, like night-ravens and bats and night-owls, futilely swarming in a shrill uproar of beaks, talons, and teeth. You are in the dark when you ascribe my death to your strength. So too the governor Pilate will be in the dark when he takes pride in possessing the power to free me or to crucify me. For even though my people and my high priests are about to hand me over to him, he would not have any power over me if it were not given to him from above. And for that very reason, those who will hand me over to him are the greater sinners. "But this is the hour and the brief power of darkness. A man who walks in the dark does not know where he is going. You also do not see or know what you are doing, and for that reason I myself will pray that you may be forgiven for what you are scheming to do to me. But not everyone will be forgiven. Blindness will not be an excuse for everyone. For you yourselves create your own darkness, you put out the light, you blind your own eyes first and then the eyes of others so that you are the blind leading the blind until both fall into a ditch. This is your short hour. This is that mad and ungovernable power which brings you armed to take an unarmed man, which brings the fierce against the gentle, criminals against an innocent man, a traitor against his lord, puny mortals against God.

"But this hour and this power of darkness are not only given to you now against me, but such an hour and such a brief power of darkness will also be given to other governors and other caesars against other disciples of mine. And this too will truly be the power of darkness. For whatever my disciples endure and whatever they say, they will not endure by their own strength or say of themselves, but conquering through my strength they will win their souls by their patience, and it is my Father's spirit that will speak in them. So too those who persecute and kill them will neither do nor speak anything of themselves. Rather, the prince of darkness, who is already coming and who has no power over me, will instill his poison in the breasts of these tyrants and tormentors and will demonstrate and exercise his strength through them for the brief time allowed him. Hence my comrades-in-arms will be struggling not against flesh and blood but against princes and powers, against the rulers of the darkness of this world, against the spiritual forces of evil in high places. Thus Nero is yet to be born, in whom the prince of darkness will kill Peter and to him will add Paul, who does not yet have that name and is still displaying his hatred of me. Through the prince of darkness other caesars and their governors will rise up against other disciples of my flock.

"But although the nations have raged and the people devised vain things, although the kings of the earth have risen up and the princes gathered together against the Lord and against His Christ, striving to break their chains and to cast off that most sweet yoke which a loving God, through His pastors, places upon their stubborn necks, then He who dwells in the heavens will laugh at them and the Lord will deride them. He sits not on a curule throne like earthly princes, raised up a few feet above the earth, but rather He rises above the setting of the sun, He sits above the cherubim, the heavens are His throne, the earth is the footstool beneath His feet, His name is the Lord, He is the king of kings and the lord of lords, a terrible king who daunts the hearts of princes. This king will speak to them in His anger, and in His rage He will throw them into confusion. He will establish His Christ, the son whom He has today begotten, as king on His holy mountain of Sion, a mountain which will not be shaken. He will cast all His enemies down before Him like a footstool under His feet. Those who tried to break His chains and cast off His yoke, He will rule against their will with a rod of iron, and He will shatter them like a potter's vessel. Against them and their instigator, the prince of darkness, my disciples will be strengthened in the Lord.

"And putting on the armor of God, their loins girt with truth, wearing the breastplate of justice, shod in preparation to preach the Gospel of peace, taking up in all things the shield of faith and putting on the helmet of salvation and the sword of the spirit, which is the word of God, they shall be clothed with power from on high. And they will stand against the snares of the devil, that is, against the soft speeches he will place on the lips of their persecutors to cajole them into leaving the way of truth. The open assaults of Satan they will also resist on the evil day: compassed about by the shield of faith, pouring forth tears in their prayers and shedding their blood in the agony of their suffering, they shall extinguish all the fiery darts hurled against them by the underlings of that monster of evil, Satan. Thus when they have taken up their cross to follow me, when they have conquered the prince of darkness, the devil, when they have trod underfoot the earthly minions of Satan, then finally, riding aloft on a triumphal chariot, the martyrs will enter into heaven in a magnificent and marvelous procession.

"But you who now give vent to your malice against me, and also that corrupt generation to come which will imitate your malice, that brood of vipers which will assail my disciples with impenitent malice similar to yours—all of you, to your everlasting infamy, will be thrust down into the dark fires of hell. But in the meantime you are permitted to demonstrate and exercise your power. Still, lest you should take too much pride in it, remember that it must shortly come to an end. For the span of time allotted to your wanton arrogance is not endless but has been shortened to the span of a brief hour for the sake of the elect, that they might not be tried beyond their strength.

"And so this hour of yours and this power of darkness are not long-lasting and enduring but quite as brief as the present moment to which they are limited, an instant of time always caught between a past that is gone and a future that has not arrived. Therefore, lest you should lose any of this hour of yours which is so short, proceed immediately to use it for your own evil purposes. Since you seek to destroy me, be quick about it, arrest me without delay, but let these men go their way."

The Flight of the Disciples

Then all the disciples abandoned Him and fled. [Mt 26:56, Mk 14:50]

From this passage it is easy to see how difficult and arduous a virtue patience is. For many can bring themselves to face certain death bravely, provided they can strike back at their assailants and give vent to their feelings by inflicting wounds on those who attack them. But to suffer without any comfort from revenge, to meet death with a patience that not only refrains from striking back but also takes blows without returning so much as an angry word, that, I assure you, is such a lofty peak of heroic virtue that even the apostles were not yet strong enough to scale it. Remembering that grand promise of theirs that they would die together with Him rather than desert Him, even they held out at least to the point of professing themselves ready to die providing that they had the chance to die fighting. And in deed as well as word Peter gave concrete evidence of this willingness by striking Malchus. But when our Savior denied them permission to fight and withheld the power to defend themselves, "they all abandoned Him and fled."

I have sometimes asked myself this question: when Christ left off praying and returned to the apostles only to find them sleeping, did He go to both groups or only to those He had brought farther along and placed nearest to Him? But when I consider these words of the evangelist, "All of them abandoned Him and fled," I no longer have any doubt that it was all of them who fell asleep. While they should have been staying awake and praying that they might not enter into temptation (as Christ so often told them to do), instead they were sleeping and thus gave the tempter an opportunity to weaken their wills with thoughtless drowsiness and make them far more inclined to fight or flee than to bear all with patience. And this was the reason that they all abandoned Him and fled. And thus that saying of Christ was fulfilled, "This night you will all be scandalized because of me," and also that prediction of the prophet, "I will strike the shepherd and the sheep of the flock will be scattered" [Zech 13:7].

But a certain young man was following Him, having only a linen cloth wrapped about his naked body, and throwing it off he fled from them naked. [Mk 14:51-52]
Just who this young man was has never been determined with certainty. Some think he was the James who was called the brother of the Lord and was distinguished by the epithet "the just." Others assert that he was the evangelist John, who always had a special place in our Lord's heart and who must have been still quite young, since he lived for so many years after Christ's death. For according to Jerome, he died in the sixty-eighth year after our Lord's passion. But there are also some ancient writers who say that this young man was not one of the apostles at all but one of the servants in the household where Christ had celebrated the Passover that night. And certainly I myself find this opinion easier to accept. Apart from the fact that I find it unlikely for an apostle to be wearing nothing but a linen cloth, and even that so loosely fastened that it could be quickly thrown off, I am inclined to this opinion first of all by the sequence of historical events and then by the very words of the account.

Now among those who think the young man was one of the apostles, the preponderance of opinion is for John. But this seems to me unlikely because of John's own words: "But Simon Peter was following Jesus, and so was another disciple. Now that disciple was known to the high priest, and he entered the courtyard of the high priest together with Jesus. But Peter was standing outside at the gate. So the other disciple, who was known to the high priest, went out and spoke to the portress and brought Peter in." Writers who assert that it was the blessed evangelist who followed Christ and fled when He was taken prisoner are faced with a slight hitch in their argument—namely, the fact that he threw off the linen cloth and fled naked. For this seems to conflict with what follows—namely, that John entered the courtyard of the high priest, that he brought Peter in (for everyone agrees that the disciple who did this was the evangelist), that he followed Christ all the way to the place of the crucifixion, and that he stood near the cross with Christ's most beloved mother (two pure virgins standing together), and that when Christ commended her to him he accepted her as his own mother from that day on.

Now there can be no doubt that at all these times and in all these places John was wearing clothes. For he was a disciple of Christ, not of the cynic sect; and therefore, though he had enough good sense not to avoid nakedness when circumstances required it or necessity demanded it, nevertheless I hardly think his virgin modesty would have allowed him to go out in public naked, for everyone to see, with no good reason at all. This difficulty they try to explain away by saying that he went somewhere else in the meantime and put on other clothes—a point I will not dispute, but it hardly seems likely to me, especially when I see in this passage that he continuously followed after Christ with Peter and that he entered the residence of Annas, the father-in-law of the high priest, together with Jesus.

Furthermore, another consideration that strongly persuades me to side with those who think that the young man was not one of the apostles but one of the servants of the inn is the sort of connection Mark makes between the apostles who ran away and the young man who stayed behind. "Then the disciples abandoned Him and all of them ran away. But a certain young man was following Him." Notice he says not that some ran away but "all of them," and that the person who (unlike them) stayed behind and followed Christ was not any one of the apostles (for all of them had already run away), but rather a "certain" young man—that is, it would seem, an unknown young man whose name Mark either did not know or thought it not worthwhile to report.

Here, then, is how I would imagine it. This young man, who had previously been excited by Christ's fame and who now saw Him in person as he was bringing in food to Christ and His disciples reclining at table, was touched by a secret breath of the Spirit and felt the moving force of charity. Then, impelled to pursue a life of true devotion, he followed Christ when He left after dinner and continued to follow Him, at a little distance, perhaps, from the apostles but still with them. And he sat down and got up again together with them until finally, when the mob came, he lost himself in the crowd. Furthermore, when all the apostles had escaped in terror from the hands of the sluggish soldiers, this young man dared to remain behind, with all the more confidence because he knew that no one as yet was aware of the love he felt for Christ. But how hard it is to disguise the love we feel for someone! Although this young man had mingled with that crowd of people who hated Christ, still he betrayed himself by his gait and his bearing, making it clear to everyone that he pursued Christ (now deserted by the others) not as a persecutor but as a devoted follower. And so when they finally noticed that the rest of Christ's band had fled and saw that this one had stayed behind and still dared to follow Christ, they quickly seized him. This act of theirs convinces me that they also intended to seize all the apostles but were so taken by surprise that they lost their chance, and thus that prophetic command of Christ "Let these men go their way" was indeed fulfilled. Christ did not intend this command to be limited to the apostles, whom He had chosen (though it was meant to apply principally to them), but He also wished to extend the riches of His kindness even more abundantly by making the command apply also to this young man, who without being summoned had followed Him of his own accord and had slipped into the holy band of His apostles. And in this way Christ displayed His own secret power more clearly and at the same time exposed the weakness of the crowd more fully, because not only did they lose through negligence the eleven apostles, whose escape distressed them very much, but also they could not even detain this one young man whom they had already seized and who was (one may conjecture) completely walled in by their ranks: for "they seized him and he threw off the linen cloth and fled from them naked." Moreover, I have not the slightest doubt that this young man, who followed Christ that night and could not be torn away from Him until the last possible moment, after all the apostles had fled—and even then it took manhandling and rough force—later took the first opportunity to return to Christ's flock and that even now he lives with Christ in everlasting glory in heaven, where I hope and pray that we will one day live with him. Then he himself will tell us who he was, and we

will get a most pleasant and full account of many other
details of what happened that night which are not contained in Scripture.

In the meantime, in order to make our heavenward
journey safer and easier, it will be of no small use for us to
gather wholesome spiritual counsels from the flight of the
disciples before they were captured and from the escape of
this young man after he was captured: these counsels will
be the provisions, as it were, for us to carry with us on the
journey. The ancient Fathers of the Church warn us not to
be so sure of our strength as to place ourselves willingly
and needlessly in danger of falling into sin. But if someone
should happen to find himself in a situation where he rec-
ognizes an imminent danger that he will be driven by force
to offend God, he ought to do what the apostles did—
avoid capture by fleeing. I do not say this to suggest that
the apostles' flight was praiseworthy, on the grounds that
Christ in His mercy (though He is indeed merciful) had
permitted them to do so because of their weakness. Far
from praising it, He had foretold it that very night as occasion of sin for them. But if we feel that our character is not
strong enough, let us all imitate this flight of theirs insofar
as we can, without sinning, flee the danger of falling into
sin. For otherwise, if a person runs away when God commands him to stand and face the danger confidently, either
for his own salvation or for that of those whom he sees
have been entrusted to his care, then he is acting foolishly
indeed, unless he does it out of concern for this present
life—no, even then he acts foolishly. For what could be
more stupid than to choose a brief time of misery over an
eternity of happiness?

But if he does it because of the future life, with the
idea that if he does not run away he may be forced to
offend God, he compounds not only his folly but also his

crime. For to desert one's post is itself a very serious crime, and if one adds to it the enormous gravity of despair, it is quite as serious as going over to the enemy's side. What worse offense could be imagined than to despair of God's help and by running away to hand over to the enemy the battle-station which God had assigned you to guard? Furthermore, what greater madness could be conceived than to seek to avoid the possible sin that may happen if you stay, by committing the certain sin of running away? But when flight entails no offense against God, certainly the safer plan is to make haste to escape rather than to delay so long as to be captured and thus fall into the danger of committing a terrible sin. For it is easy and (where allowable) safe to run away in time, but it is difficult and dangerous to fight.

On the other hand, the example of this young man shows us what sort of person can afford to hold his ground longer with less danger and can easily escape from the hands of his captors if he should happen to be taken. For although this young man stayed behind after all the others and followed Christ so long that they laid hands on him and held him, nevertheless, because he was not dressed in various garments but wore only a simple linen cloth—and even that not sewn together or buttoned on, but thrown carelessly over his naked body in such a way that he could easily shake it off—this young man suddenly threw off the cloth, leaving it there in the hands of his captors, and fled from them naked—taking the kernel, as it were, and leaving them holding the shell. What is the figurative meaning of this? What else but this: just as a potbellied man slowed down by his fat paunch or a man who goes around wearing a heavy load of clothes is hardly in a condition to run fast, so too the man who is hemmed in by a belt full of money-bags is hardly able to escape when troubles sud-

denly descend on him and put him in a bind. Neither will a
man run very fast or very far if his clothing, however light
it may be, is so tightly laced and knotted that he cannot
breathe freely. For a man who is wearing a lot of clothing
but can get rid of it quickly will find it easier to escape than
a man who is wearing only a little but has it tied around
his neck so tightly that he has to carry it with him wherever he runs. One sees rich men—less often, it is true, than I
would like—but still, thank God, one sometimes sees
exceedingly rich men who would rather lose everything
they have than keep anything at all by offending God
through sin. These men have many clothes, but they are
not tightly confined by them, so that when they need to
run away from danger, they escape easily by throwing off
their clothes. On the other hand we see people—and far
more of them than I would wish—who happen to have
only light garments and quite skimpy outfits and yet have
so welded their affections to those poor riches of theirs that
you could sooner strip skin from flesh than separate them
from their goods. Such a person had better get going while
there is still time. For once someone gets hold of his
clothes, he will sooner die than leave his linen cloth
behind. In summary, then, we learn from the example of
this young man that we should always be prepared for
troubles that arise suddenly, dangers that strike without
warning and might make it necessary for us to run away;
to be prepared, we ought not to be so loaded with various
garments, or so buttoned up in even one, that in an emer-
gency we are unable to throw away our linen cloth and
escape naked.

Now anyone who is willing to devote a little more
attention to this deed of the young man can see that it
offers us another teaching, even more forceful than the
first. For the body is, as it were, the garment of the soul.

The soul puts on the body when it comes into the world and takes off the body when it leaves the world at death. Hence just as the clothes are worth much less than the body, so too the body is far less precious than the soul. Thus to give away the soul to buy the body is the same kind of raving lunacy as to prefer the loss of the body to the loss of a cloak. Concerning the body, Christ did indeed say, "Is not the body worth more than its clothing?" But concerning the soul He was far more emphatic: "What does it profit you if you gain the whole world but suffer the loss of your soul? Or what will a man give in exchange for his soul? But I say to you, my friends, do not be afraid of those who kill the body, and after that have nothing more that they can do. But I will show you the one to be afraid of. Fear Him who, after He has killed, has the power to cast into hell. Yes, I say to you, fear Him." Thus the example of this young man warns us about what sort of clothing for our souls our bodies ought to be when we are faced with such trials: they should not be obese from debauchery and flabby from dissolute living but thin like the linen cloth, with the fat worked off by fasting; and then we should not be so strongly attached to them that we cannot willingly cast them off when God's cause demands it. This is the lesson which that young man teaches us; when he was in the clutches of wicked men, he preferred to leave his linen cloth behind and flee from them naked rather than be forced to do or say anything which might impugn the honor of Christ.

In a similar way, another young man who lived long before this one, the holy and innocent patriarch Joseph, left to posterity a notable example, teaching that one should flee from the danger of unchaste defilement no less than if it were an attempted murder. Because he had a handsome face and was a fine figure of a man, the wife of Potiphar, in whose house he was the chief servent, cast her eyes on him and fell passionately in love with him. She was so carried away by the raving madness of her desire that she not only offered herself freely and shamelessly to the young man by her glances and words, enticing him to overcome his aversion, but also, when he refused, she went so far as to clutch his garment in her hands and presented the shameful spectacle of a woman wooing a man by force. But Joseph, who would rather have died than commit such a horrible sin and who also knew how dangerous it is to engage the embattled forces of Venus at close quarters and that against them the surest victory is flight—Joseph, I say, left his cloak in the hands of the adulteress and escaped by dashing out of doors.

But as I was saying, to avoid falling into grave sin we must throw off not merely a cloak or gown or shirt or any other such garment of the body but even the garment of the soul, the body itself. For if we strive to save the body by sin, we destroy it and we also lose the soul. But if we patiently endure the loss of the body for the love of God, then just as the snake sloughs off its old skin (called, I think, its "senecta") by rubbing it against thorns and thistles and, leaving it behind in the thick hedges, comes forth young and shining, so too those of us who follow Christ's advice and become wise as serpents [Mt 10:16] will leave behind on earth our old bodies, rubbed off like a snake's old skin among the thorns of tribulation suffered for the love of God, and will quickly be carried up to heaven, shining and young and never more to feel the effects of old age.

The Capture of Christ

Then they came up and laid hands on Jesus. The cohort and the tribune and the servants of the Jews seized Jesus and, holding Him fast, they bound Him and took Him first to Annas. For he was the father-in-law of Caiaphas. But it was Caiaphas who had advised the Jews that it is expedient that one man die for the people. [Jn 18:12-14] *And all the priests, scribes, Pharisees, and elders gathered together.* [Mt 26:57, Mk 14:53]

Exactly when they first laid hands on Jesus is a point on which the experts disagree. Among the interpreters of the gospel accounts, which agree on the fact but vary in their way of presenting it (for one anticipates, another goes back to pick up a detail omitted earlier), some commentators follow one opinion, others another, though none of them impugn the historical truth of the accounts or deny that an opinion differing from their own may be the correct one. For Matthew and Mark relate the events in such an order as to allow the conjecture that they laid hands on Jesus immediately after Judas' kiss. And this is the opinion adopted not only by many celebrated doctors of the church but also approved by that remarkable man John Gerson, who follows it in presenting the sequence of events in his work entitled *Monotessaron* (the work which I have generally followed in enumerating the events of the passion in this discussion).

But in this one place I have departed from him and followed those interpreters (and they too are celebrated authorities) who are persuaded by very probable inferences from the accounts of Luke and John to adopt the opinion that only after Judas had given his kiss and returned to the cohort and the Jews, after Christ had thrown down the cohort merely by speaking to them, after the ear of the high priest's servant had been cut off and restored, after the other apostles had been forbidden to fight and Peter (who had already begun to fight) had been rebuked, after Christ had once more addressed the Jewish magistrates who were present at that time and had announced that they now had permission to do what they had not been able to do before (to take Him captive), after all the apostles had escaped by running away, after the young man who had been seized but could not be held had saved himself by his active and eager acceptance of naked-ness—only then, after all these events, did they lay hands on Jesus.

More's Collection of Scriptural Quotes and Reflections

If your enemy should fall, do not be glad; let not your heart rejoice in his downfall, lest perhaps God should see and be displeased [Prov 24:17-18].

Do not return a curse for a curse [1 Pt 3:9].

Pray for those who persecute you [Mt 5:44].

Do not cool yourself in every breeze, and do not walk on every road. Be steadfast in the way of the Lord and in the truth of your judgment. Be meek in hearing the word of God that you may understand it, and make your reply with wisdom. If you understand the matter, give your neighbor an answer; but if not, put your hand over your mouth, lest you be caught saying something silly and be confounded. Never in your life be called a tale-bearer, and do not be tripped up and confounded by your tongue. But the tale-bearer shall have hatred and enmity and reproach [Sir 5:11-17].

All flesh is grass and all its glory is like the flower of the field. The grass has withered and its flower has fallen. But the word of the Lord endures forever [1 Pt 1:24-25, quoting Is 40:6-8].

Whatever light and momentary affliction we now bear prepares for us an immeasurable and eternal weight of glory on high, while we contemplate not the things that are seen but the things that are not seen. For the things that are seen are temporal, but those that are not seen are eternal [2 Cor 4: 17- 18].

The sufferings of the present time are not worthy to be compared to the glory to come which will be revealed in us [Rm 8:18].

Eye has not seen nor ear heard nor has it entered into the heart of man, what things God has prepared for those who love Him [1 Cor 2:9].

Cast your thoughts upon God and He will support you [Ps 55:22].

Beloved, do not be startled at the trial by fire that is taking place among you to prove you, as if something strange were happening to you; but rejoice, insofar as you share in the sufferings of Christ, that you may also rejoice with exultation in the revelation of His glory [1 Pt 4:12-13].

Let those who suffer according to the will of God commend their souls to a faithful Creator [1 Pt 4:19].

Good men should be ashamed to be more timid in good deeds than wicked men are in wicked deeds. For one may hear thieves saying that a man is a coward to refuse seven years of pleasure to avoid a half hour of hanging, and should not a Christian man be ashamed to lose eternal life and happiness rather than be willing to suffer a quick death a little sooner, for he knows that he will have to suffer death a little later anyway and that unless he repents he will fall from a temporal death to an eternal death, one full of more grievous torments than any death whatever.

If you despair in the day of distress, your courage will be diminished [Prov 24:10].

Peter walked erect on the water with confidence, but when the wind rose and he began to lose his confidence and be afraid, he immediately began to sink. But when he called to Christ for help, Christ reached out His hand, saying, "O you of little faith, why did you doubt?" [Based on Mt 14:29-31.]

Christ was tempted not once but three times, and also afterwards. For as Luke testifies, the tempter left Him "until the time" [Lk 4:13].

God is faithful and does not permit you to be tempted beyond what you can bear, but with the temptation also gives a way out [1 Cor 10:13].

Consider it nothing but joy, my brothers, when you fall into various trials, knowing that the trying of your faith produces patience. But let your patience have its perfect work, that you may be whole and perfect [Jms 1:2-4].

Whoever wishes to be my disciple, let him take up his cross and follow me [Mt 16:24, Mk 8:34, Lk 9:23 and 14:27].

They have crucified their flesh with its vices and desires [Gal 5:24].
The world is crucified to me and I to the world [Gal 6:14].

Strong as death is love [Cant 8:6].

I long to be dissolved and to be with Christ [Phil 1:23].

For me to live is Christ and to die is gain [Phil 1:21].

As the hind longs for springs of water, so my soul longs for you, O God. My soul has thirsted for God, the living spring. When shall I come and appear before the face of God? [Ps 43:1-2].

I say to you, my friends, do not be afraid of those who can kill the body and after that have nothing more that they can do. But I will show you whom you ought to be afraid of. Fear him who, when he has killed, has the power to cast into hell. Yes, I say to you, fear him [Lk 12:4-5].

Your adversary the devil goes about like a roaring lion, seeking someone to devour [1 Pt 5:8]. Bernard: I give thanks to that great Lion of the tribe of Judah [Rv 5:5]; he can roar but he cannot bite. However much he may threaten, let us not be beasts that an empty roar should lay us low. For that man is truly a beast, truly lacking reason, who is so fainthearted that fear alone makes him yield, who even before the battle is conquered simply by an exaggerated notion of the effort to come and is laid low not by a weapon but by a war-trumpet. "For you have not yet resisted as far as blood," says that vigorous leader who knew that the roar of this lion is futile [Heb 12:4]; and another leader says, "Resist the devil and he will flee from you" [Jms 4:7]. "Resist him, steadfast in the faith" [1 Pt 5:9].

He chose a glorious death over a hateful life [2 Macc 6:19]. If a man saves his life by offending God, he will find the life he has saved in this way to be hateful. For if you save your life in this way, on the very next day you yourself will find your life hateful and you will be very sorry indeed that you did not suffer death the day before. For you will remember that death still awaits you, though you do not know what sort it will be nor how quickly it will come. And you have good reason to fear that this delayed death will be followed by the torments of hell, where men will long to die and death will flee from them [Rv 9:6], whereas the death you fled from would have been followed by the eternal glory of heaven.

Your adversary the devil goes about like a raging lion, seeking someone to devour [1 Pt 5:8]. This lion is the prince of this world, nor is there any power on earth like him. The strongest and most savage of men, compared with this lion, would be like a Maltese lapdog. A roaring and rapacious lion [Ps 22:13] is attacking me, seeking to devour me, and do I have time to give even a thought to the bite of a little dog? If a person could see even one of these demons who are waiting for us in great numbers to torture us eternally, he would consider the combined threats of all mortals a mere trifle by comparison with the fear inspired by that one devil. And how much less would he think of these threats if he could see the heavens opened and Jesus standing there as blessed Stephen saw Him? [Acts 7:55-56]. How foolish is it to avoid a temporary death by incurring an eternal one! And not even to avoid the temporary one, but merely to put it off for a little while! For if you avoid death for the time being, can you always be as successful? Will you die at another time without pain? Perhaps even you are threatened by the same danger that Christ declared to the rich man who promised himself a long life: "Fool, this night they will snatch from you your soul" [Lk 12:20]. But this much you know for certain, that you must die sometime and, considering the brevity of human life, you cannot live long. Finally, you are doubtless aware that when the fatal disease arrives and your anguish begins to grow worse in the throes of death, you will wish you had died long before when you could have saved your soul, no matter how excruciating the death might have been. Therefore you should not be so desperately afraid of what might happen, since you know that a little later you will wish that that very thing had happened.

He is affected with sadness... bad health....

The sadness that is according to God produces repentance that surely tends toward salvation, but the sadness of this world produces death [2 Cor 7:10].

My soul is sad even unto death [Mt 26:38 and Mk 14:34].

For I would not have you ignorant, brothers, of the tribulation which came upon us in Asia, for we were burdened beyond measure, so that we were weary even of life [2 Cor 1:8].

As the sufferings of Christ abound in us, so also through Christ does our comfort abound [2 Cor 1:5].
Part of the sufferings of Christ was fear and sadness. Then,

because of His weariness and fear, in the anguish of His agony, drops of His blood dripped on the ground. [Based on Lk 22:44.]

Isaiah predicts that [those who] abandon [hope in] God [and take refuge in] human assistance [will perish] together with their assistance [Is 31:3]. Thus perished King Saul, who, murmuring impatiently and despairing of God's help because he had not been heard immediately, went over to consult a witch, although formerly he had commanded by a public edict that all witches should be punished [1 Sam 28:5-25 and 1 Chr 10:13-14].

Naked you came into the world [and you will take] nothing away with you [1 Tm 6:7 and Eccles 5:14].

The Lord gave, the Lord has taken away. As it pleased the Lord, so has it been done [Job 1:21].

... of Christ ... this man [was led] who in all things ... nor once opened His mouth [Acts 8:32, Is 53: 7] ... [not] a word of complaint or excuse or threat or curse [1 Pt 2:23] would He speak against those cursed dogs [Ps 22:16], but His very last act was to pour forth a word of blessing on His enemies, such as was never heard from the beginning of the world [Jn 9:32]: Father, forgive them for they know not what they do [Lk 23:34].

Blessed be God and the Father of our Lord Jesus Christ, who according to His mercy has begotten us again, through the resurrection of Jesus Christ from the dead, unto a living hope, unto an incorruptible inheritance, undefiled and unfading, reserved in heaven for you, who are guarded by the power of God through faith unto salvation, the salvation made ready to be revealed in the last days. In this you rejoice, though you must now be saddened for a little while by various temptations, that the trial of your faith may be far more precious than gold which is tried by fire, that it may be discovered unto praise and glory and honor at the revelation of Jesus Christ. Him, though you have not seen, you love. In Him, though you do not see Him now, you believe, and believing, you will rejoice with a joy inexpressible and triumphant, receiving as the final issue of your faith the salvation of your souls [1 Pt 1:3-9].

Fear God. Honor the king. Servants, be subject to your masters in all fear, not only to the good and moderate, but also to the bad-tempered. For this is indeed a grace, if for consciousness of God anyone endures sorrows, suffering unjustly. For how is it a grace if when you sin and are buffeted you endure it? But if when you do right you suffer patiently, this is indeed a grace in the eyes of God. For to this you have been called, because Christ too suffered for us, leaving us an example that we might follow in His footsteps. "He committed no sin, nor was deceit found in His mouth" [Is 53:9]. When He was cursed, He did not curse. When He suffered, He did not threaten but handed Himself over to him who judged Him unjustly. He Himself bore our sins in His body on the cross that we, having died to sin, might live to justice. By His bruises we were healed [1 Pt 2:17-24].

Be all of one mind in the faith, compassionate, loving your

brothers, merciful, modest, humble, not returning evil for evil or curse for curse, but contrariwise, blessing. For to this you were called that you might inherit a blessing [1 Pt 3:8-9].

Who is there to harm you if you are zealous for what is good? But even if you suffer anything for the sake of justice, blessed are you. But have no fear of their fear that you may not be troubled, but in your hearts declare the holiness of the Lord, always ready to satisfy anyone who asks you the reason for the hope that is in you. But do so with modesty and fear, having a good conscience, so that those who unjustly blame your good behavior in Christ may be put to shame for the detractions they have brought against you. For it is better, if such is the will of God, that we should suffer for doing good than for doing evil. For Christ, too, once died for our sins, the just for the unjust, that He might offer us to God as men dead indeed in the flesh, but brought to life in the spirit [1 Pt 3:13-18].

But the end of all things will draw near. Therefore, be prudent and watchful in prayers. But above all, have a constant mutual charity among yourselves, for charity covers a multitude of sins [1 Pt 4:7-8].

Beloved, do not be startled at the trial by fire that is taking place among you to prove you, as if something strange were happening to you; but rejoice, insofar as you share in the sufferings of Christ, that you may also rejoice with exultation in the revelation of His glory. If you are reproached in the name of Christ, blessed shall you be because the honor, glory, and power of God and His Spirit

rest upon you. Let none of you suffer as a murderer or
thief or a slanderer or as one who covets what belongs to
others. But if he suffers as a Christian, let him not be
ashamed, but let him glorify God under that name. For the
time is at hand for the judgment to begin with the household of God. But if it begins first with us, what will be the
end of those who do not believe the Gospel? For if the just
man will barely be saved, what will happen to the wicked
man and the sinner? Therefore let those who suffer according to the will of God commend their souls to a faithful
Creator by doing good deeds [1 Pt 4:12-19].

And you became imitators of us and of the Lord, receiving
the word in great tribulation, with joy of the Holy Spirit [1
Thess 1:6].

As a helper, then, we exhort you not to receive the grace of
God in vain. For he says, "In an acceptable time I have
heard you and in the day of salvation I have helped you"
[Is 49:8]. Behold, now is the acceptable time. Behold, now is
the day of salvation. Giving offense to no one, so that our
ministry may not be blamed, let us rather show ourselves
in all things to be the ministers of God: in much patience in
tribulations, in hardships, in distress; in blows, in prisons,
in tumults; in labors, in sleepless nights, in fasting; in inno-
cence, in knowledge, in long-suffering; in kindness, in the
Holy Spirit, in unfeigned charity; in the word of truth, in
the power of God, with the armor of justice on the right
hand and on the left: in honor and dishonor; in evil report
and good report; as deceivers and yet truthful; as unknown
and yet well known; as dying, and behold, we live; as chas-
tised but not killed; as sorrowful yet always rejoicing; as

poor yet enriching many; as having nothing yet possessing all things [2 Cor 6:1-10].

God, who commanded light to shine out of darkness, has Himself shone in our hearts to give enlightenment concerning the knowledge of the glory of God, shining in the face of Jesus Christ. But we carry this treasure in vessels of clay, to show that the abundance of power is God's and not ours. In all things we suffer tribulation but we are not distressed; we are shaken but we are not destitute; we suffer persecution but we are not forsaken; we are humiliated but not put to shame; we are cast down but we do not perish; always bearing about in our body the dying of Jesus so that the life also of Jesus may be made manifest in our bodies. For we the living are always being handed over to death for the sake of Jesus, so that the life also of Jesus may be made manifest in our mortal flesh [2 Cor 4:6-11].

For we know that if the earthly house in which we dwell be destroyed, we have a building from God, a house not made by human hands but eternal in the heavens. For even in this present state we groan, longing to be clothed over with that habitation of ours which is from heaven, if indeed we shall be found clothed and not naked. For even we who are in this tent groan and are burdened, because we do not wish to be unclothed but rather clothed over, that what is mortal might be swallowed up by life. Now He who made us for this very thing is God, who gave us the Spirit as its pledge. Always full of courage, then, and knowing that while we are in the body we are exiled from the Lord—for we walk by faith and not by sight—we have the courage and the greatest willingness to be even more

126   THE SADNESS OF CHRIST

exiled from the body and to be in the presence of God. And therefore we strive, whether in the body or out of it, to please Him. For all of us must be made manifest before the tribunal of Christ, so that each one may receive what he has won through the body, according to his works, whether good or evil [2 Cor 5:1-10].

For you know the graciousness of our Lord Jesus Christ—how being rich, He became poor for your sakes, that by His poverty you might become rich [2 Cor 8:9]. He does not say "having been rich" He became poor, but "being rich" He took on poverty without losing His riches—inwardly rich, outwardly poor, having the hidden riches of divinity but appearing in the poverty of humanity. All of us, then, become rich by believing in the poor Christ. Therefore, let no poor man in his hut look down on himself. Rich in his conscience, he sleeps more securely on the ground than the man rich in gold does on his regal coverlet. And so do not be afraid to come like a poor beggar before Him who, clothing Himself in our poverty, enriched us by impoverishing Himself.

If anyone does not obey our word by this letter, note that man and do not associate with him, that he may be put to shame. And do not regard him as an enemy, but admonish him as a brother. But may the God of peace Himself give you everlasting peace in every place [2 Thess 3:14-16].

How good is the God of Israel to those who are upright of heart. But my feet almost wavered, my steps almost slipped [Ps 73:1-2].

Direct my steps according to your word, and do not let any injustice rule over me [Ps 119:133].

O God, you know my folly, and my offenses are not hidden from you. Let not those who are waiting for you be put to shame because of me, O Lord, Lord of hosts. Let those who seek you not be confounded because of me, O God of Israel [Ps 69:5-6].

Blessed be the Lord, the God of Israel, who alone does wondrous things. And blessed be the name of His majesty forever, and the whole earth shall be filled with His majesty. So be it! So be it! [Ps 72:18-19].

Tribulation and distress have found me out; your commandments are my meditation [Ps 119:143].

Imploring Divine Help Against Temptation, While Scorning Demons Through Hope and Confidence in God

A Prayer Composed of the Psalms by Sir Thomas More While a Prisoner in the Tower of London

Psalm 3   O Lord, how many are my adversaries! Many rise up against me! [the soul recovering from sin]   Many are saying of me, "There is no salvation for him in God." But you, O Lord, are my shield; my glory, you lift up my head! When I lie down in sleep, I wake again, for the Lord sustains me. [one who rises from sin]*   I fear not the myriads of people arrayed against me on every side. [scorning the demons]

Psalm 5   O Lord, because of my enemies, guide me in your justice; make straight your way before me. For in their mouth there is no sincerity; their heart teems with treacheries. Their throat is an open grave. [against the plots of the demons]   Judge them, O God; let them fall by their own devices; for their many sins, cast them out because they have rebelled against you.

But let all who take refuge in you be glad and exult forever. Protect them, that you may be the joy of those who love your name. For you, O Lord, bless the just man; you surround him with the shield of your good will.

---

*These bracketed comments are those More wrote in the margins of his psalter.

Psalm 7   O Lord, my God, in you I take refuge; save me
from all my pursuers and rescue me [against
the spirits of evil] , lest I become like the lion's prey, to be
torn to pieces, with no one to rescue me. Rise up, O Lord,
in your anger, rise against the fury of my foes. [against
demons]   Let the enemy pursue and overtake me; let him
trample my life to the ground and lay my glory in the dust.
He will bend and aim his bow, prepare his deadly
weapons against them, and use fiery darts for arrows. He
who conceived iniquity and was pregnant with mischief
brings forth failure. He has opened a hole, he has dug it
deep, but he falls into the pit which he has made. [against
the demon]   His mischief shall recoil upon his own head;
upon the crown of his head his violence shall rebound. I
will give thanks to the Lord for His justice, and sing praise
to the name of the Lord Most High.

Psalm 4   As soon as I lie down, I fall peacefully asleep,
for you alone, O Lord, bring security to my
dwelling.

Psalm 9   Have pity on me, O Lord; see how I am
afflicted by my foes. They trust in you who
cherish your name, for you forsake not those who seek
you, O Lord. The Lord is a stronghold for the oppressed,
a stronghold in times of distress. Why, O Lord, do you
stand aloof? Why hide in times of distress? For the needy
shall not always be forgotten, nor shall the hope of the
afflicted forever perish. Rise, O Lord! O God, lift up your
hand! Forget not the afflicted! On you the unfortunate
man depends; of the fatherless you are the helper. The
desire of the afflicted you hear, O Lord; strengthening

their hearts, you pay heed.

Psalm 11   The Lord is in His holy temple; the Lord's
throne is in heaven. His eyes behold, His
searching glance is on mankind.

Psalm 12   "Because they rob the afflicted and the
needy sigh, now will I arise," says the
Lord.

Psalm 7   O Lord, my God, in you I take refuge; save
me from all my pursuers and rescue me.
[against the spirits of evil]

Psalm 13   How long, O Lord, will you utterly forget
me? How long will you hide your face from
me? [The one who has scruples in confession and is not
satisfied in his own soul should pray this psalm.]   How
long shall I harbor sorrow in my soul, grief in my heart
day after day? How long will my enemy triumph over
me? Look, answer me, O Lord, my God!

Give light to my eyes that I may not sleep in death, lest
my enemy say, "I have overcome him," lest my foes rejoice
at my downfall though I trusted in your kindness. Let my
heart rejoice in your salvation; let me sing of the Lord, "He
has been good to me."

Psalm 16   Keep me, O God, for in you I take refuge; I
say to the Lord, "My Lord are you. Apart
from you I have no good."

Psalm 17   My steps have been steadfast in your

paths, my feet have not faltered. [He asks that he not waver in temptation.] Show your wondrous kindness, O savior of those who flee from their foes to refuge at your right hand.

Psalm 16   I set the Lord ever before me; with Him at my right hand I shall not be disturbed. [comfort in tribulation] Therefore my heart is glad and my soul rejoices; my body, too, abides in confidence.

Psalm 18   You indeed, O Lord, give light to my lamp; O my God, you brighten the darkness about me; for with your aid I run against an armed band, and by the help of my God I leap over a wall. God's way is unerring, the promise of the Lord is fire-tried; He is a shield to all who take refuge in Him. For who is God except the Lord? Who is a rock, save our God?

Psalm 22   But I am a worm, not a man; the scorn of men, despised by the people. [when suffering disgrace] All who see me scoff at me; they mock me with parted lips, they wag their heads.

You have been my guide since I was first formed, my security at my mother's breast. To you I was committed at birth, from my mother's womb you are my God. Be not far from me, for I am in distress; be near, for I have no one to help me. But you, O Lord, be not far from me; O my help, hasten to aid me. [against demons]

Psalm 23   Even though I walk in the dark valley, I fear no evil, for you are at my side with your rod and your staff that give me courage. [confidence in tribulation]

Psalm 25   To you I lift up my soul, O Lord, my God.
In you I trust; let me not be put to shame,
let not my enemies exult over me. [demons] No one who
waits for you shall be put to shame. The sins of my youth
and my frailties remember not; [for sins] in your kindness remember me, because of your goodness, O Lord. For
your name's sake, O Lord, you will pardon my guilt, great
as it is. [for sins] My eyes are ever toward the Lord, for
He will free my feet from the snare. [from sin or prison,
tribulation] Relieve the troubles of my heart, and bring
me out of my distress. Put an end to my affliction and my
suffering, and take away all my sins.

Psalm 27   The Lord is my light and my salvation;
whom should I fear? [confidence] The
Lord is my life's refuge; of whom should I be afraid?
Though an army encamp against me, my heart will not
fear; though war be waged upon me, even then will I trust.
One thing I ask of the Lord; this I seek: to dwell in the
house of the Lord all the days of my life, that I may gaze on
the loveliness of the Lord and contemplate His temple.
Hear, O Lord, the sound of my call; have pity on me, and
answer me. Of you my heart speaks; you my glance seeks;
your presence, O Lord, I seek. Hide not your face from me;
do not in anger repel your servant. You are my helper: cast
me not off; forsake me not, O God my savior. I believe that
I shall see the bounty of the Lord in the land of the living.
[hope and confidence] Wait for the Lord with courage; be
stouthearted, and wait for the Lord. [patience]

Psalm 28   To you, O Lord, I call; O my Rock, be not deaf to me, lest, if you heed me not, I become one of those going down into the pit.

Psalm 30   Sing praise to the Lord, you His faithful ones, and give thanks to His holy name. For His anger lasts for a moment; a lifetime, His good will. At nightfall, weeping enters in, but with the dawn, rejoicing. When you hid your face, I was terrified. [tribulation] To you, O Lord, I cried out; with the Lord I pleaded: "What gain would there be from my lifeblood, from my going down into the grave?

Psalm 31   In you, O Lord, I take refuge; let me never be put to shame. In your justice rescue me, incline your ear to me, make haste to deliver me! Be my rock of refuge, a stronghold to give me safety. You are my rock and my fortress; for your name's sake you will lead and guide me. You will free me from the snare they set for me, for you are my refuge. [against the snares of the demons] Into your hands I commend my spirit; you will redeem me, O Lord, O faithful God.

Have pity on me, O Lord, for I am in distress; with sorrow my eye is consumed; my soul also, and my body. For my life is spent with grief and my years with sighing; my strength has failed through affliction, and my bones are consumed. For all my foes I am an object of reproach, a laughingstock to my neighbors, and a dread to my friends; they who see me abroad flee from me. [in times of disgrace and danger] I am forgotten like the unremembered dead; I am like a dish that is broken. I hear the whispers of the crowd, that frighten me from every side, as they consult together against me, plotting to take my life. But my trust is in you, O Lord; I say, "You are my God." In your hands is my destiny. Let your face shine upon your servant; save me in your kindness. O Lord, let me not be put to shame, for I call upon you. How great is the goodness, O Lord, which you have in store for those who fear you. [consolation for the soul in tribulation]

Psalm 33   But see, the eyes of the Lord are upon those who fear Him, upon those who hope for His kindness, to deliver them from death and preserve them in spite of famine. Our soul waits for the Lord, who is our help and our shield, for in Him our hearts rejoice; in His holy name we trust. May your kindness, O Lord, be upon us who have put our hope in you.

Psalm 34   Look to Him that you may be radiant with joy, and your faces may not blush with shame.
The angel of the Lord encamps around those who fear Him, and delivers them. Taste and see how good the Lord is; happy the man who takes refuge in Him. Fear the Lord, you His holy ones, for nought is lacking to those who fear Him. The great grow poor and hungry; but those who seek the Lord want for no good thing. The Lord is close to the brokenhearted, and those who are crushed in spirit He saves.

Psalm 36   The children of men take refuge in the shadow of your wings. They have their fill of the prime gifts of your house; from your delightful stream you give them to drink. For with you is the fountain of life, and in your light we see light.

Psalm 38   O Lord, in your anger punish me not, in
                 your wrath chastise me not;   [a good
psalm for seeking forgiveness]   for your arrows have sunk
deep in me, and your hand has come down upon me.
There is no health in my flesh because of your indignation;
there is no wholeness in my bones because of my sin, for
my iniquities have overwhelmed me; they are like a heavy
burden, beyond my strength.

Noisome and festering are my sores because of my
folly, I am stooped and bowed down profoundly; all the
day I go in mourning, for my loins are filled with burning
pains; there is no health in my flesh. I am numbed and
severely crushed; I roar with anguish of heart.

O Lord, all my desire is before you; from you my
groaning is not hid. My heart throbs; my strength forsakes
me; the very light of my eyes has failed me. My friends and
my companions stand back because of my affliction; my
neighbors stand afar off. Men lay snares for me, seeking
my life; they look to my misfortune, they speak of ruin,
treachery they talk of all the day. But I am like a deaf man,
hearing not, like a dumb man who opens not his mouth.
[So should the meek man act during tribulation; he should
neither speak proudly nor throw back words badly spoken, but should bless them that speak badly and suffer
willingly, either for the sake of justice if he has merited it
or for the sake of God if he has not.]   I am become like a
man who neither hears nor has in his mouth a retort,
because for you, O Lord, I wait; you, O Lord my God, will
answer when I say, "Let them not be glad on my account
who, when my foot slips, glory over me."

For I am very near to falling, and my grief is with me always. Indeed, I acknowledge my guilt; I grieve over my sin. But my undeserved enemies are strong; many are my foes without cause. Those who repay evil for good harass me for pursuing good. Forsake me not, O Lord; my God, be not far from me! Make haste to help me, O Lord my salvation!

Psalm 39   I said, "I will watch my ways, so as not to sin with my tongue; I will set a curb on my mouth." [abstain from abusive language] While the wicked man was before me, I kept dumb and silent; I refrained from rash speech. But my grief was stirred up; hot grew my heart within me; in my thoughts, a fire blazed forth. I spoke out with my tongue:

Let me know, O Lord, my end and what is the number of my days, that I may learn how frail I am. A short span you have made my days, and my life is as nought before you; only a breath is any human existence. A phantom only, man goes his ways; like vapor only are his restless pursuits; he heaps up stores and knows not who will use them.

And now, for what do I wait, O Lord? In you is my hope. From all my sins deliver me; a fool's taunt let me not suffer.

I was speechless and opened not my mouth, because it was your doing; take away your scourge from me; at the blow of your hand I wasted away. With rebukes for guilt you chasten man; you dissolve like a cobweb all that is dear to him; only a breath is any man. Hear my prayer, O Lord; to my cry give ear; to my weeping be not deaf! For I am but a wayfarer before you, a pilgrim like all my fathers.

Turn your gaze from me, that I may find respite ere I depart and be no more.

Psalm 40   Happy the man who makes the Lord his trust; who turns not to idolatry or to those who stray after falsehood. How numerous have you made, O Lord my God, your wondrous deeds! And in your plans for us there is none to equal you; should I wish to declare or to tell them, they would be too many to recount.

Withhold not, O Lord, your compassion from me; may your kindness and your truth ever preserve me. For all about me are evil beyond reckoning; my sins so overcome me that I cannot see; they are more numerous than the hairs of my head, and my heart fails me. Deign, O Lord, to rescue me; O Lord, make haste to help me.

But may all who seek you exult and be glad in you, and may those who love your salvation say ever, "The Lord be glorified." Though I am afflicted and poor, yet the Lord thinks of me. You are my help and my deliverer; O my God, hold not back!

Psalm 42   As the hind longs for the running waters, so my soul longs for you, O God. [Happy is he who can say this from his soul.] Athirst is my soul for God, the living God. When shall I go and behold the face of God? Those times I recall, now that I pour out my soul within me, when I went with the throng and led them in procession to the house of God, amid loud cries of joy and thanksgiving, with the multitude keeping festival. Why are you so downcast, O my soul? Why do you sigh within me? [in tribulation] Hope in God! For I shall again be thanking Him, in the presence of my savior and my God.

Within me my soul is downcast; so will I remember you from the land of the Jordan and of Hermon, from Mount Misar. Deep calls unto deep in the roar of your cataracts; all your breakers and your billows pass over me. By day the Lord bestows His grace, and at night I have His song, a prayer to my living God. I sing to God, my Rock: "Why do you forget me? Why must I go about in mourning, with the enemy oppressing me?" It crushes my bones that my foes mock me, as they say to me day after day, "Where is your God?" Why are you so downcast, O my soul? Why do you sigh within me? Hope in God! For I shall again be thanking Him, in the presence of my savior and my God.

Psalm 46   God is our refuge and our strength, an ever-present help in distress. [confidence in God against tribulation] Therefore we fear not, though the earth be shaken and mountains plunge into the depths of the sea; though its waters rage and foam and the mountains quake at its surging. The Lord of hosts is with us; our stronghold is the God of Jacob.

There is a stream whose runlets gladden the city of God, the holy dwelling of the Most High. God is in its midst; it shall not be disturbed; God will help it at the break of dawn.

Psalm 51   Have mercy on me, O God, in your goodness; in the greatness of your compassion wipe out my offense. Thoroughly wash me from my guilt and of my sin cleanse me. For I acknowledge my offense, and my sin is before me always: "Against you only have I sinned, and done what is evil in your sight"—that you may be justified in your sentence, vindicated when you condemn. Indeed, in guilt was I born, and in sin my mother conceived me; behold, you are pleased with sincerity of heart, and in my inmost being you teach me wisdom. Cleanse me of sin with hyssop, that I may be purified; wash me, and I shall be whiter than snow. Let me hear the sounds of joy and gladness; the bones you have crushed shall rejoice. Turn away your face from my sins, and blot out all my guilt. A clean heart create for me, O God, and a steadfast spirit renew within me. Cast me not out from your presence, and your holy spirit take not from me. Give me back the joy of your salvation, and a willing spirit sustain in me. I will teach transgressors your ways, and sinners shall return to you. Free me from blood guilt, O God, my saving God; then my tongue shall revel in your justice. O Lord, open my lips, and my mouth shall proclaim your praise. For you are not pleased with sacrifices; should I offer a holocaust, you would not accept it. My sacrifice, O God, is a contrite spirit; a heart contrite and humbled, O God, you will not spurn.

Be bountiful, O Lord, to Sion in your kindness by rebuilding the walls of Jerusalem; then shall you be pleased with due sacrifices, burnt offerings and holocausts; then shall they offer up bullocks on your altar.

Psalm 55   Hearken, O God, to my prayer; turn not away from my pleading; give heed to me, and answer me. My heart quakes within me; the terror of death has fallen upon me. [in tribulation] Fear and trembling come upon me, and horror overwhelms me, and I say, "Had I but wings like a dove, I would fly away and be at rest." Cast your care upon the Lord, and He will support you.

Psalm 62   Only in God is my soul at rest; from Him comes my salvation. [patience in tribulation, or I will not commit such a sin again]   He only is my rock and my salvation, my stronghold; I shall not be disturbed at all. How long will you set upon a man and all together beat him down as though he were a sagging fence, a battered wall?

Only in God be at rest, my soul, for from Him comes my hope. [patience]   He only is my rock and my salvation, my stronghold; I shall not be disturbed. With God is my safety and my glory, He is the rock of my strength; my refuge is in God. Trust in Him at all times, O my people! Pour out your hearts before Him; God is our refuge!

One thing God said; these two things which I heard: that power belongs to God, and yours, O Lord, is kindness; and that you render to everyone according to his deeds.

Psalm 63   O God, you are my God whom I seek; for you my flesh pines and my soul thirsts like the earth, parched, lifeless and without water. [longing for God]   Thus have I gazed toward you in the sanctuary to see your power and your glory, for your kindness is a greater good than life; my lips shall glorify you. [in tribulation and fear of death]

Thus will I bless you while I live; lifting up my hands, I will call upon your name. As with the riches of a banquet shall my soul be satisfied, and with exultant lips my mouth shall praise you. I will remember you upon my couch, and through the night watches I will meditate on you; that you are my help, and in the shadow of your wings I shout for joy. My soul clings fast to you; your right hand upholds me.

But they shall be destroyed who seek my life, they shall go into the depths of the earth; they shall be delivered over to the sword, and shall be the prey of jackals. The king, however, shall rejoice in God; everyone who swears by Him shall glory, but the mouths of those who speak falsely shall be stopped.

Psalm 67   May God have pity on us and bless us; may He let His face shine upon us. So may your way be known upon earth; among all nations, your salvation. May the peoples praise you, O God; may all the peoples praise you!

May the nations be glad and exult because you rule the peoples in equity; the nations on the earth you guide. May the peoples praise you, O God; may all the peoples praise you!

The earth has yielded its fruits; God, our God, has blessed us. May God bless us, and all the ends of the earth fear Him.

How to Treat Those Who Wrong Us

A Godly Instruction, Written by Sir Thomas More, Knight, While He Was Prisoner in the Tower of London in 1534

Bear no malice or evil will to any man living. For either the man is good or wicked. If he is good and I hate him, then I am wicked.

If he is wicked, either he will amend and die good and go to God, or live wickedly and die wickedly and go to the devil. And then let me remember that if he be saved, he will not fail (if I am saved too, as I trust to be) to love me very heartily, and I shall then in like manner love him.

And why should I now, then, hate one for this while who shall hereafter love me forevermore, and why should I be now, then, an enemy to him with whom I shall in time be coupled in eternal friendship? And on the other side, if he will continue to be wicked and be damned, then is there such outrageous eternal sorrow before him that I may well think myself a deadly cruel wretch if I would not now rather pity his pain than malign his person. If one would say that we may with good conscience wish an evil man harm lest he should do harm to other folk who are innocent and good, I will not now dispute upon that point, for that root has more branches to be well weighed and considered than I can now conveniently write (having no other pen than a coal). But truly will I give counsel to every good friend of mine that unless he be put in such a position as to punish an evil man in his charge by reason of his office, he should leave the desire of punishing to God and to such other folk who are so grounded in charity and so fast cleaved to God that no secretly malicious or cruel affection can creep in and undermine them under the cloak of a just and a virtuous zeal. But let us that are no better than men of a mean sort ever pray for such merciful amendment in other folk as our own conscience shows us that we have need of in ourselves.

On Saving One's Life

*Written by Sir Thomas More
While He Was a Prisoner
In the Tower of London, in 1534*

Whoever saves his life in such a way that he displeases God shall soon afterwards, with no little grief, find his life thoroughly displeasing. For if you so save your life, you shall on the next day so mortally hate your life that you will be wholeheartedly sorry you did not lose your life the day before. For that you certainly must die you will surely remember, but how or how soon, that you do not know at all. And you have just cause to fear that the delay of that death may well ensure the everlasting torments in hell, where men shall sorely long to die and death shall flee from them; whereas by enduring that death you so much abhorred, there should have undoubtedly followed the everlasting joys of heaven.

What folly is it, then, for you to avoid this temporal death and thereby fall into peril of purchasing for yourself eternal death? Even then you do not escape your temporal death, but only perhaps delay it for a while.

For suppose you think you can for that while avoid the danger of death. Are you therefore sure either to continue your life forever or at another time to die and feel no pain? No. Rather, the same might easily happen to you that happened to the rich man who assured himself that he would live many more years. To this man Christ said, "This night, you fool, shall they take from you your life" [Lk 12:20]. And again, of these two things you can be sure: that you shall die once, and (for so quickly man's life here passes away) that you cannot live here for long.

Finally, I suppose you can have no doubt at all that, when the time will come when you will lie sick on your deathbed and will begin to feel the painful pangs of death so dreadfully drawing on, then you will heartily wish, for the saving of your soul, that you had died a most sharp and cruel death many a day before. Indeed, then have you no cause to fear so greatly that to happen which, as you know well yourself, you would soon wish to have happened to you before. Whoever suffer any trouble or adversity, according to the will of God, must wholly commit their souls into the hands of God, their trusty and faithful Creator.

"Be not discouraged, my well-beloved brethren," says St. Peter, "by reason of the extreme persecution that is among you (which is sent to you as a proof of your patience) as though some strange thing were befallen you. But inasmuch as you are partakers of Christ's pains and passion, wholeheartedly rejoice, that you may likewise rejoice at the revelation of his glory" [1 Pt 4:12-13].

Well may good men be ashamed to have less courage to do good than evil men have to do evil. For one may hear thieves say without hesitation that he has a faint stomach who will not risk a half an hour's hanging for seven years of pleasure. And what a shame would it be, then, for a Christian to be content to lose everlasting life and bliss rather than suffer a short death somewhat before his time — especially since he is well assured that suffer he shall within a while and that, unless he repent in time, he shall fall straight from his temporal death into an eternal death so horrible and painful that it far exceeds all other kinds of death.

If it were possible to behold with bodily eyes one of those grisly fiends which in such great numbers daily look and long for us, so that they can torment us forever in hell, the fear of him alone would make a man consider of no importance all the terrible threats that anyone could imagine. And how much less would he regard them if he might possibly see heaven open and Jesus Christ standing there, as did the blessed Saint Stephen [Acts 7:55-56].

"Your adversary the devil," says St. Peter, "like a roaring lion runs about, seeking whom he may devour" [1 Pt 5:8]. But hear what St. Bernard says: "I humbly thank the mighty Lion of the tribe of Judah; well may this lion roar, but bite me he cannot." No matter how much he threatens us, let us not be such beastly cowards that just at his rough roaring we fall flat on the ground.

For a very beast is he, having no reason indeed, who is either so feeble-spirited that he gives up out of fear alone or is so shaken by a vain imagination of the pain that he may happen to suffer that at the bare blast of the trumpet — before the battle begins — he is clean overthrown without any stroke at all. "You have not resisted as yet to the shedding of your blood," says that valiant captain who knew right well that the roaring of this lion was nothing to be minded [Heb 12:4]. And another says, "Stand firm against the devil, and he will flee from you" (Jms 4:7].

"Stand firm I say, with a strong and steadfast faith" [1 Pt 5:9] for Isaiah gave us warning that those who, having no hope of God's help, fly for succor to man's help shall, both themselves and their helpers with them, come to utter confusion [Is 31:1,3].

So came King Saul to nought, who, because he was

not immediately heard at his pleasure by God, mur-
mured, grudged, and distrusted God and so ended up
seeking counsel of a witch — though he himself, for the
punishment of all witches, had given without exception
such a precise commandment before [1 Kgs 28:2-25; 1
Chr 10:13-14].

My firm hope is that He who so dearly bought me will
not, without my own damnable fault, lose me to His most
malicious enemy.

*

A Meditation on Detachment

Written by Sir Thomas More, Knight,
While a Prisoner in the Tower of London, 1534

Give me thy grace, good Lord,
To set the world at nought;

To set my mind fast upon thee,
And not to hang upon the blast of men's mouths;

To be content to be solitary,
Not to long for worldly company;

Little by little utterly to cast off the world,
And rid my mind of all the business thereof;

Not to long to hear of any worldly things,
But that the hearing of worldly phantasies may
    be to me unpleasant;

Gladly to be thinking of God,
Piteously to call for His help;

To lean unto the comfort of God,

Busily to labor to love Him;
To know my own vileness and wretchedness,
To humble and meeken myself under the mighty
    hand of God;

To bewail my sins passed;
For the purging of them, patiently to suffer adversity;

Gladly to bear my purgatory here;
To be joyful of tribulations;

To walk the narrow way that leads to life,
To bear the cross with Christ;

To have the last thing in remembrance,
To have ever before my eye my death that is ever at hand;

To make death no stranger to me,
To foresee and consider the everlasting fire of hell;

To pray for pardon before the judge come,
To have continually in mind the passion that Christ
    suffered for me;

For His benefits unceasingly to give Him thanks,
To buy the time again that I before have lost;

To abstain from vain conversations,
To eschew light foolish mirth and gladness;

Recreations not necessary—to cut off;
Of worldly substance, friends, liberty, life and all,
    to set the loss as nothing

for the winning of Christ;
To think my greatest enemies my best friends;
For the brethren of Joseph could never have done him
    so much good with their love and favor
        as they did him with their malice and hatred.

These attitudes are more to be desired of every man
    than all the treasure of all the princes and kings,
        Christian and heathen,
            were it gathered and laid together all upon
            one heap.

A Prayer Before Dying

A Prayer Composed by Sir Thomas More, Knight,
After He Was Condemned to Die.

(Our Father, Hail Mary, the Creed.)

O Holy Trinity, the Father, the Son, and the Holy Spirit—three equal and coeternal Persons, and one almighty God—have mercy on me, a vile, abject, abominable, sinful wretch. I meekly acknowledge before Your High Majesty my long-continued sinful life, from my very childhood to the present.

In my childhood, in this point and that point....

After my childhood, in this point and that point..., and so forth by every age.

Now, good gracious Lord, as You give me Your grace to acknowledge them, so give me Your grace not only in words but also in my heart, with very sorrowful contrition, to repent them and utterly to forsake them. And forgive me those sins also in which by my own fault, through evil affections and evil custom, my reason is so blinded with sensuality that I cannot discern them as sins. And illumine, good Lord, my heart, and give me Your grace to know them and to acknowledge them, and forgive me my sins negligently forgotten, and bring them to my mind with

151

grace so that I can be purely confessed of them.

Glorious God, give me from henceforth the grace, with little respect towards the world, so to set and fix firmly my heart upon You that I may say with Your blessed apostle Saint Paul, "The world is crucified to me, and I to the world. For to me to live is Christ and to die is gain. I wish to be dissolved and be with Christ" [Gal 6:14, Phil 1:21-23].

Give me the grace to amend my life and to have an eye to my end without grudge of death, which to them that die in You, good Lord, is the gate to a prosperous life.

Almighty God, "Teach me to do Your will. Make me run in the scent of Your unguents. Take my right hand, and lead me in the right path because of my enemies. Draw me after You. With a muzzle and bridle restrain my jaws when I do not draw near to You" [Ps 143:10, Cant 1:3, Ps 73:23, 27:11, 32:9].

O glorious God, all sinful fear, all sinful sorrow and pensiveness, all sinful hope, all sinful mirth and gladness take from me. And on the other side, concerning such fear, such sorrow, such heaviness, such comfort, consolation, and gladness as shall be profitable for my soul, "Deal with me according to Your great goodness, O Lord" [Ps 119:124].

Good Lord, give me the grace in all my fear and agony to have recourse to that great fear and wonderful agony that You, my sweet Savior, had at the Mount of Olivet before Your most bitter passion, and in the meditation thereof to conceive spiritual comfort and consolation profitable for my soul.

Almighty God, take from me all vainglorious attitudes, all appetites of my own praise, all envy, covetousness, gluttony, sloth and lechery, all wrathful affections, all appetite of revenging, all desire or delight of other folks' harm, all pleasure in provoking any person to wrath and anger, all delight of rebuking or insulting any person in their affliction and calamity.

And give me, good Lord, a humble, lowly, quiet, peaceable, patient, charitable, kind, tender, and merciful mind, with all my works and all my words and all my thoughts to have a taste of Your holy blessed Spirit.

Give me, good Lord, a full faith, a firm hope, and a fervent charity; a love for You, good Lord, incomparably above the love of myself; and that I love nothing to Your displeasure, but everything for the sake of You.

Give me, good Lord, a longing to be with You, not for the avoiding of the calamities of this wretched world, nor so much for the avoiding of the pains of purgatory, nor of the pains of hell either, nor so much for the attaining of the joys of heaven, in respect to my own benefit, but for a genuine love for You.

And bear me, good Lord, Your love and favor, which my love for You (no matter how great) could not, but for Your great goodness, deserve.

And pardon me, good Lord, that I am so bold to ask such great petitions, being such a vile and sinful wretch and so unworthy to attain the lowest. But yet, good Lord, such they be as I am bound to wish, and should be nearer the effectual desire of them if my many sins were not the hindrance. From which, O glorious Trinity, grant of Your goodness to wash me with that blessed blood that issued out of Your tender body (O sweet Savior Christ) in the diverse torments of Your most bitter passion.

Take from me, good Lord, this lukewarm fashion—or rather, key-cold manner—of meditation, and this dullness in praying to You. And give me warmth, delight, and quickness in thinking upon You, and give me Your grace to long for Your holy sacraments, and especially to rejoice in the presence of Your very blessed body, sweet Savior Christ, in the holy sacrament of the altar, and duly to thank You for Your gracious visitation there, and, at that high memorial, with tender compassion to remember and consider Your most bitter passion.

Make each of us, good Lord, a devout participant of that holy sacrament this day, and every day make us all living members, sweet Savior Christ, of Your holy mystical body, Your Catholic Church.

Deign, O Lord, on that day to preserve us without sin.

Have mercy upon us, O Lord, have mercy upon us.

Let Your mercy, O Lord, be upon us, just as we have hoped in You.

In You, O Lord, have I hoped; let me not be confounded for eternity.

Pray for us, holy mother of God, that we may be made worthy of the promises of Christ.

For Friends:

Almighty God, have mercy on N. and N., etc. (with special meditation and consideration of every friend, as godly affection and occasion requires).

For Enemies:

Almighty God, have mercy on N. and N., etc., and on

all that bear me evil will and would harm me. And by such easy, tender, and merciful means as Your infinite wisdom can best devise, grant that their faults and mine may both be amended and redressed; and make us saved souls in heaven together, where we may ever live and love together with You and Your blessed saints. O glorious Trinity, grant this for sake of the bitter passion of our sweet Savior Christ. Amen.

Lord, give me patience in tribulation, and grace in everything to conform my will to Yours, that I may truly say: "Thy will be done on earth as it is in heaven" [Mt 6:10].

The things, good Lord, that I pray for, give me the grace to labor for. Amen.